D0948397

BUILDING A BROADER MARKET

BUILDING A BROADER MARKET

Report of

The Twentieth Century Fund Task Force
on the Municipal Bond Market

Background paper by
RONALD W. FORBES
and JOHN E. PETERSEN

McGraw-Hill Book Company

New York   St. Louis   San Francisco   Auckland   Bogotá
Düsseldorf   Johannesburg   London   Madrid   Mexico
Montreal   New Delhi   Panama   Paris   São Paulo   Singapore
Sydney   Tokyo   Toronto

THE TWENTIETH CENTURY FUND is a research foundation engaged in policy-oriented studies of economic, political, and social issues and institutions. It was founded in 1919 by Edward A. Filene, who made a series of gifts that now constitute the Fund's assets.

Library of Congress Cataloging in Publication Data

Twentieth Century Fund. Task Force on the Municipal
   Bond Market.
   Building a broader market.

   Includes bibliographical references.
   1. Municipal bonds—United States.   I. Forbes,
Ronald W.   II. Petersen, John E.   III. Title.
HG4952.T85   1976   332.6'323   76-28368
ISBN 0-07-065629-0
ISBN 0-07-065630-4 pbk.

Contents

Foreword

The report of the Task Force on the Municipal Bond Market is the second examination of this critical institutional mechanism to be undertaken under the auspices of the Twentieth Century Fund. Earlier, another distinguished group of authorities, some of whom also participated in this study, deliberated over the issue of municipal bond credit ratings and recommended the creation of a national data bank to compile and analyze pertinent information on the condition of state and local governmental borrowers. That first report, *The Rating Game*, which still has great relevance, was published before the great turmoil that afflicted the municipal bond market as a result of the financial crises confronting New York City and New York State. Following that great upheaval, the present Task Force was constituted to consider what should be done to improve the overall structure of the market so that it could function effectively and equitably in serving local governmental borrowers, investors, and, of course, the taxpayer who, in the long run, must pay the costs of municipal indebtedness.

This second report, together with its background paper, makes it clear that the municipal bond market requires restructuring to meet the needs of both borrowers and investors. The present inadequacies of the market, however, cannot be blamed for the plight of New York City and other municipalities whose financial difficulties are such that they no longer have normal access to the market. Even if all of the recommendations made by the Task Force are adopted, resulting in a broader and stronger market than now exists, the plight of the nation's aging and financially ailing cities would still be with us. Such cities require special emergency assistance that no market mechanism can provide. Although the Task Force dealt with the special problems confronting the nation's near-bankrupt cities, it devoted most of its deliberations to ways and means of improving the operations of the market.

Even if reform and restructuring of the market are unable to help New York City, they can be of substantial benefit to state and local governments seeking funds for public purposes. Such restructuring and reform are also beneficial to investors—the purchasers of municipals. Finally, a broader and stronger market serves the public as a whole, particularly the taxpayers and users of the facilities built by local governments with borrowed funds.

The Fund has sponsored two Task Forces in this area because the functioning of the municipal bond market is of vital public importance. Unless it operates effectively and equitably, access to credit and the cost of credit may pose serious problems for all borrowers, resulting in undue burdens on taxpayers or in sacrifice of needed public facilities. But equitable and effective operation of the market calls for a thorough understanding of the market. The Task Force makes a convincing argument for a great many different measures to improve the workings of the market, and it makes recommendations that, taken together, would do much to provide a market capable of meeting the challenges of the next decade and beyond.

Although the Task Force did not reach unanimous agreement on each proposal, it was in accord on most measures. Given the diverse and firmly held positions of the participants, the extent and depth of their agreement was a signal achievement. I am delighted to express my appreciation to the members of the Task Force for their dedication and devotion and for their effort to reach agreement on critical issues. A special tribute is due to Ray Garrett and Philip Hoff, the cochairmen of the Task Force, who exhibited both good sense and instinct in presiding over the deliberations. Their work was aided by Ronald Forbes and John Petersen, who wrote the background paper and served as the rapporteurs for the Task Force.

The Fund is grateful to all of them for their comprehensive report on the municipal bond market, which merits much more public attention and debate than it has received.

M. J. Rossant, DIRECTOR
The Twentieth Century Fund
July 1976

Members of the Task Force

Ivan Allen, Jr.
Former Mayor of the City of
  Atlanta
Chairman of the Board, Ivan
  Allen Company
Atlanta, Georgia

Ray Garrett, Jr. Esq.
Cochairman
Former Chairman of the
  Securities and Exchange
  Commission
Partner, Gardner, Carton
  and Douglas
Chicago, Illinois

Philip H. Hoff, *Cochairman*
Former Governor of Vermont
Partner, Hoff, Bryan, Quinn
  and Jenkins
Burlington, Vermont

Richard Leone
State Treasurer
Trenton, New Jersey

Frank E. Morris
President, Federal Reserve
  Bank of Boston
Boston, Massachusetts

Walter W. Niebling
Vice-President, Merrill
  Lynch, Pierce, Fenner and
  Smith, Inc.
New York

Joseph A. Pechman
Director of Economic Studies,
  The Brookings Institution
Washington, D.C.

Neal R. Peirce
Contributing Editor, The
  National Journal
Washington, D.C.

Leland S. Prussia, Jr.
Executive Vice-President and
  Cashier, Bank of America,
  NT&SA
San Francisco, California

Report of the Task Force

INTRODUCTION

The municipal bond market—the nationwide network in which states, cities, and local government agencies borrow funds for public purposes—has experienced increasing difficulty in recent years. Like other markets, it has been adversely affected by the shifts in national monetary policy and the abrupt change in the temper of the times. But it also has been made shakier by the precipitous decline in the demand for tax-exempt municipal issues on the part of major institutional buyers, particularly the commercial banks, whose purchases had fueled the enormous growth of the municipal market in the last decade. Yet the supply of municipals in the form of relatively new and unseasoned instruments, such as the so-called moral obligation bond, and the number of new functions, such as pollution control, multiplied. As a result, the market clearly had faced strains and tensions before it was confronted with New York's financial crisis last fall.

Fortunately, the market managed to survive—but not easily and not without cost. The inability of the nation's largest city to raise funds directly was largely due to its own lack of creditworthiness, the consequence of many years of misguided fiscal machinations. New York's difficulties, however, drew attention to the limitations of the market and the structural weaknesses that have handicapped it. Even some creditworthy borrowers were forced to pay more for money last fall or could not find all the money they sought, which meant a greater burden on taxpayers and users of new facilities. In a few cases, new facilities could not be built.

This Task Force, which was established following the trials and tribulations that shook the market last fall, has not been concerned primarily with the plight of New York, although it has recognized the need to provide emergency credit assistance to those municipalities, mainly the nation's aging cities whose economic prospects have changed so drastically, who cannot raise adequate funds from the market. Rather, the Task Force devoted itself to the deep-rooted problems of inefficiency and inequity that penalize creditworthy borrowers.

As the members of the Task Force represent a broad spectrum of political viewpoints and institutional affiliations, their discussions reflected widely diverging and strongly held views on the proper role of government and the nature of market forces. It proved impossible to achieve unanimity in all of the recommendations of the Task Force. Nevertheless, the Task Force was united in its conviction that the municipal bond market, the machinery most commonly used by local government units for raising capital to build and operate such public facilities as schools and hospitals, dams and toll roads, mass transit systems and sewage disposal units, required fundamental restructuring and reform.

The objective of the Task Force was to provide a broader and deeper municipal market, one which will better serve state and local governments needing funds for public facilities and investors seeking relatively safe and marketable securities. Consequently, the Task Force took a number of different approaches in its recommendations. But all of them are designed to improve the functions of the market to ensure that it can maintain a steady and reliable flow of capital from investors, both individual and institutional, to state and local borrowers for appropriate public purposes.

Strengthening the market is not only essential to investors and government borrowers but also is vital to taxpayers and the public at large, since they must ultimately repay the borrowed funds in the form of taxes or user charges. Because the municipal market now relies exclusively on the appeal of the tax-exempt interest that is paid to holders of state and local government obligations, these obligations attract only certain classes of investors, those who are seeking tax-exempt income.

The market must be broadened and thereby deepened through an increase in the marketability and attractiveness of government obligations to all types of investors.

In addition, the market would be strengthened by some restrictions on the supply of municipal obligations. The Task Force believes that some issues that are now marketed are not really qualified as appropriate borrowings in the public interest and do not merit tax exemption or subsidy. The elimination of such issues would be another important step in improving the workings of the market.

The Task Force also pondered ways and means in which to improve the quality of credit, thus giving borrowers greater access to the market at less cost. Finally, it sought to reconcile the needs of investors and the interests of the public in the financing of public projects.

Investors are entitled to some grounds for confidence that they will receive the promised return on their investments. Governments issue bonds ostensibly to finance projects that serve public needs, and the justification for the tax-exempt status of their obligations is precisely that. The question of accountability arises when the issuing agency is not directly answerable to the public. Investors may well view proposals, for example, to make the tenure of authority boards of directors coterminous with that of state governors as opening the door to patronage and corruption. But the public must have some means of influencing the use that is made of its credit.

What follows is an agenda for the restructuring of this market designed to strengthen its operations in the long run and to benefit borrowers, investors, and the public alike.

BROADENING THE MARKET AND IMPROVING ITS EFFICIENCY

The Task Force recommends that the federal government give state and local governments the option of using a taxable debt instrument, *on which the federal government would pay part of the interest, as a means of obtaining financing.**

The taxable bond option represents the single most effective way of broadening and stabilizing the market for state and local borrowing while preserving the healthy insulation of state and local governments from federal involvement. Given such an option, governmental issuers could tap the larger markets for taxable debt securities now dominated by institutional investors, namely, pension funds, nonprofit and charitable trusts, and life insurance companies. Because their liabilities are long-term and relatively predictable and their receipts are stable, these institutions are natural buyers of obligations with long-term maturity and fixed income. But they are largely tax-exempt themselves and hence have little need for tax-exempt income. The taxable bond option would relieve the tax-exempt market of its present reliance on banks and fire and property insurance companies, which are volatile buyers of long-term tax-exempt securities.

The purpose of the tax exemption is to enable municipal issuers to keep their interest rates lower than those on taxable securities. (Investors in high tax brackets can achieve a greater return from a low interest rate that is not taxed than from a high interest rate that is taxed.) But when money is tight, issuers must offer higher yields in order to attract individual investors into the long-term tax-exempt market. Under these conditions, tax exemption becomes inefficient, and the issuers of taxable securities complain that it distorts the equity of the tax system. The taxable bond option would help to relieve

---

*Comment: Messrs. Garrett, Niebling, and Robinson oppose the taxable bond option. In their view, as a practical matter, the affairs of municipal issuers that take advantage of the option cannot be insulated from federal involvement, regardless of how unconditional and "automatic" the availability of federal payments may be in the initial legislation. Once conditions on availability begin to be imposed, by statute or administrative discretion, local autonomy will be circumscribed. And if taxable bonds become the only possible financing vehicle, the localities will lose autonomy. At the very best, this form of federal subsidy, in their opinion, should be deferred until the beneficial effects of the other measures recommended by the Task Force have had a chance to be evaluated.

these upward pressures and assist not only those governmental borrowers electing direct subsidies but also those issuing traditional tax-exempt securities.

Although the federal government might well recoup a large proportion of the subsidy payments in increased tax receipts, the Task Force does not view the taxable bond option as a revenue-raising mechanism for the Treasury. Rather, it is a highly leveraged form of assistance that should lower the costs to state and local borrowers by some large multiple of the net cost to the Treasury.

The Task Force recommends that the taxable bond option be designed to broaden the market for municipal securities and to bring its interest rate into line with those in the taxable securities market. The federal subsidy should therefore be a fixed percentage of the interest cost on securities sold on a taxable basis. Views on the appropriate percentage level for the subsidy differ.* The Task Force believes that the rate should be 35 to 40 percent.† The option program and the federal interest payments themselves must be straightforward and guaranteed. Ideally, the option should be available on any securities issue that can be sold on a tax-exempt basis.

To be effective, the option must remain completely voluntary. And the system of federal payments under the option must be simple enough to provide the same ease of market access currently found in the tax-exempt market. The subsidy's operation should not be crippled by regulations that would discourage its use and deny its benefits to the largest possible number of issuers. The Task Force, concluded that as long as the tax-exempt option remains, the possibility of federal interference with state and local affairs is remote. The

---

*On June 17, 1976, the Department of Housing and Urban Development proposed regulations to implement a taxable bond option for state housing finance and development agencies. These regulations are designed to implement the authority granted in the 1974 Housing and Community Development Act and would provide an interest subsidy of 33 1/3 percent on the taxable securities issued by these agencies.

†*Comment:* Mr. Prussia believes that a subsidy of 30 to 35 percent is more appropriate than one of 35 to 40 percent.

Mr. Pechman believes that a 50 percent subsidy should be considered.

option seems useful as a simple means of expanding investment interest in municipal securities as long as its use would be optional and the rate of the federal subsidy would be fixed at a level that did not distort borrowing choices. However, because the taxable bond option would use existing marketing channels and would be generally available to governmental borrowers, problems arising from misuses of credit or inefficient issuance procedures would not be solved. Recommendations dealing with these problems appear later in this report.

Other steps can also be taken to broaden the market for municipal bonds. Increasing efficiency and competition in the financial institutions that handle these securities can widen their appeal.*

The Task Force believes that mutual funds and other regulated investment companies should be permitted to pass through tax-exempt interest income to their shareholders and that the U.S. Internal Revenue Code should be amended to this effect.

The present restrictions in the tax code against the pass-through of tax-exempt interest income creates an unnecessary and inequitable obstacle to the purchase of state and local government securities by those investors who prefer or need the assistance, convenience, and diversity of managed mutual investment funds.

Until the present time, small investors have had to use unit investment trusts to obtain portfolio diversification and professional selection of tax-exempt investments. But such trusts still do not possess all the characteristics of the managed investment fund. Thus, the market for municipal securities is needlessly constricted, and interest rates on tax-exempt securities are higher in order to overcome their marketing handicap.†

Comment: Messrs. Pechman and Prussia observe that the taxable bond option will lower the marginal (after-tax) return of state and local securities to high-income investors and encourage these investors to seek other high-return investments, increasing the supply of venture capital and thus strengthening the equity capital market.

Messrs. Hoff and Morris endorse this view.

†A mutual fund that qualifies as a "regulated investment company," as defined in the Internal Revenue Code, is not itself subject to tax on its income

A type of managed municipal bond portfolio with tax-exemption flow-through, in the form of a limited partnership, has recently been approved by the Internal Revenue Service (IRS). However, adapting the limited partnership to this purpose is cumbersome; the Internal Revenue Code should be amended to make available the corporate form. Experience will have to determine whether the investment performance of a managed portfolio will prove sufficiently superior to that of the fixed portfolio—long available through the unit investment trust—to compensate for the management fee.

Facilitating the use of the mutual fund form to invest in a diversified and managed portfolio of tax-exempt municipal bonds can expand the overall market for tax-exempt securities. Mutual funds can play an important role when institutional interest wanes and the tax-exempt market relies heavily on the individual investor.

*The Task Force recommends that, for federal income tax purposes, nonbank underwriters be allowed to deduct from gross income, as a business expense, the interest charges paid on monies borrowed to finance the carrying of tax-exempt securities.**

Because they perform the same function, both bank and nonbank underwriters should be accorded parallel treatment under the tax code for their interest expenses. Financing municipal bond underwriting operations through the use of borrowed funds is a long-established and necessary way of conducting the business of investment banking. Commercial banks are permitted to deduct the interest paid on time de-

provided it distributes at least 90 percent of its income to its shareholders annually. However, even if the mutual fund's income consists of interest on tax-exempt bonds, the distributions to shareholders are taxable as dividends, provided that the fund is a corporation or a "taxable association." Efforts to organize a fund with a managed portfolio of tax-exempt bonds (as contrasted with the fixed, "unmanaged" portfolio of a unit investment trust) have, in the opinion of the Internal Revenue Service, all resulted in taxable associations until recently where the limited partnership form has been used.

Comment: Messrs. Leone and Pechman believe that there should be equity in the treatment of bank and nonbank underwriters. But they think a better road to achieving such equity would be not to allow either type of underwriter to deduct interest costs.

Mr. Hoff endorses this view.

posits and other borrowed funds, which are a part of the pool of funds used to support bank underwriting and purchases of tax-exempt securities. If nonbank underwriters were permitted a similar tax deduction of interest expense, they would be under less pressure to price new issues at yields high enough to ensure a rapid sellout of inventories and spreads sufficient to compensate for the higher effective interest cost of carrying the bonds. This recommendation not only would promote tax equity between nonbank underwriters and commercial banks but also should tend to lower tax-exempt interest rates marginally.

*The Task Force also recommends that commercial banks be allowed to underwrite state and local government revenue bonds.** *

Commercial banks are excluded by the Glass-Steagall Act from underwriting and trading state and local government revenue bonds. In many cases, revenue bonds differ only slightly from tax-supported obligations. As a class, they represent an important form of government security and are perfectly acceptable as bank portfolio investments, yet the exclusion continues and restricts the market for these bonds.

The Task Force grants that on individual transactions the expected savings will be small; in the aggregate, however, the savings could be appreciable. In any event, banks should be allowed to underwrite all valid tax-exempt offerings on the grounds of equity and to promote competition that might lower the overall cost of public borrowing.

REDUCING THE SUPPLY OF BONDS

The Task Force recommends elimination of the use of tax-exempt industrial development bonds as financing for plant and equipment for privately owned businesses, except in very rare instances clearly serving the public interest.

*Comment: Messrs. Garrett, Niebling, and Robinson do not wish to join in this recommendation on the grounds that the long-term competitive effects have not been adequately determined.

Present legislation and current Internal Revenue Service rules elaborately define and impose complex restrictions on industrial development bonds. But many public officials are pressing for the removal of such restrictions primarily as a means of generating more employment.

Between 1969, when the Tax Reform Act was passed, and 1975, sales of development bonds to finance plant and equipment grew from almost nothing to a reported $500 million a year. Because many regional economies are recovering only slowly from the severe recession of 1974–75, the industrial development bond is being promoted with renewed vigor as a stimulus for local economic growth.

The public benefits of tax-exempt financing for this purpose are dubious. In the view of the Task Force, the opportunity to issue industrial development bonds encourages a questionable form of competition between states and localities. Much of the competitive potential of the technique is eliminated by the general availability of such assistance throughout the state. Moreover, the subsidy provided by lower tax-exempt interest rates extends only to the capital costs of economic development and hence does little to encourage labor-intensive projects.

The Task Force is not aware of any evidence that such tax-exempt-financed investment increases overall investment and employment. Indeed, this form of financing promotes a misallocation of resources because it provides an incentive for investments that otherwise have little justification. The benefits of industrial development bonds are weighted heavily in favor of private enterprise and the stockholders of the assisted firms.

Of course, in a few special cases, the use of public credit to facilitate certain types of private investment that serve important public purposes and would not otherwise be undertaken may be appropriate. One such case is the redevelopment of land and the rehabilitation of urban core areas. In many older central cities, the costs and risks involved in the acquisition and development of sites for new industrial facilities may be so onerous that private entrepreneurs will not assume them without some public sharing of risks and costs. For these reasons, the Task Force does not recommend an absolute prohibition against the use of tax-exempt securities in the financing of developmental activities that involve private interests.

The Task Force believes that tax-exempt financing should remain available for area development and redevelopment. But such financing must be used responsibly and only where the larger public interest controls and predominates.

The Task Force also recommends that the federal government enact legislation to eliminate the use of tax-exempt financing of pollution control facilities for private enterprise and make alternative methods of assistance available.

Between 1972 and 1975, sales of pollution control bonds grew from virtually nothing to more than $2.5 billion a year in public financings and perhaps that much again in private placements. This new competition for funds has adversely affected all tax-exempt borrowers, increasing the long-term tax-exempt rate by an estimated 10 to 20 basis points (precise figures are unobtainable), imposing an additional borrowing cost annually of $30 million to $60 million on long-term state and local borrowers.

The Task Force recognizes that special incentives to reduce the costs to industry of environmental control are probably necessary.* But, although the public at large may have to share these costs, tax-exempt financing is not an efficient means of inducing industry to protect the environment. The bonds sold are generally of long-term maturity, the least efficient segment of the tax-exempt market. Moreover, private firms do not have equal access to tax-exempt financing; companies that have the greatest need of assistance, because they are small or have weak credit characteristics, are the ones least likely to benefit from tax-exempt financing.†

Comment: Mr. Pechman believes that industry should conform with environmental control legislation without special tax incentives. If incentives are regarded as necessary by the Congress, direct assistance through federal expenditures would be much more efficient than indirect assistance through tax preferences. It is time to call a halt to the proliferation of "tax expenditures" and this is a good place to draw the line.

†In June 1976, President Ford signed legislation (S. 2498) authorizing

As a practical matter, the Task Force is persuaded that such tax-exempt financing cannot be eliminated unless alternative forms of pollution control subsidy are available. One such alternative, favored by many firms, is a restructuring of the investment tax credit for pollution control expenditures. For example, a 10 percent investment tax credit confers approximately the same economic benefits on a given firm as does a tax-exempt bond issue for the same purpose. A tax-credit system would also be less time-consuming and costly than the marketing of debt issues.

In some situations, jointly developed private-public pollution control projects may be more economical than separate facilities. The Task Force believes that such economies should be encouraged. Private enterprise need not be excluded from pollution control projects with tax-exempt financing as long as the governmental benefit from such joint ventures clearly justifies the use of tax-exempt financing.

The Task Force has grappled with the complexities of the Internal Revenue Code provisions regarding the allowable users and uses of tax-exempt financing. Of course, these complexities reflect the diversity of state and local governmental borrowers and evolving notions of what constitutes public purpose. The Task Force has concluded that the tax-exempt status of industrial development and pollution control bonds is both hurtful to the market and inefficient and recommends its elimination.

We also believe that, at a minimum, tax-exempt financing should not be available for the acquisition of facilities on behalf of private profit-making firms; such financing enables them both to borrow at a low cost and to charge depreciation of facilities against their taxable income. A practical method of curtailing the use of tax exemption by profit-making entities would be to eliminate the tax deduction for depreciation charges on those facilities purchased or constructed through the use of tax-exempt funds.

the Small Business Administration (SBA) to provide federal guarantees on leases that secure tax-exempt industrial revenue bonds issued for pollution control purposes on behalf of small business. Regulations implementing this legislation are being developed by SBA.

The Task Force recognizes that a laundry-list approach to reform only perpetuates the complexities in the tax code's definitions of legitimate tax-exempt borrowers and legitimate purposes. Constant fine tuning to permit one borrower or use but deny another borrower or use is both administratively cumbersome and conceptually unsatisfactory.

The Task Force recommends a general reexamination of the federal and state legislation and regulations that govern the scope of permissible users and uses of tax-exempt financing. The federal government should revise its regulations to avoid inequity and inefficiency in granting admission to the privileges of immunity of interest income from the federal tax collector. It also should simplify such laws and restrict tax exemption to the financing of facilities owned by governments or by borrowing entities that are genuine subdivisions of and accountable to governmental bodies. The ultimate objective should be to improve the accountability of entities that borrow on behalf of the public. Although such entities may need some insulation from the tumult and uncertainties of day-to-day political activities, the electorate as such must have a means of communicating with and influencing those that act in its behalf. The risk that governmental facilities may perform somewhat less efficiently because of occasional political interference is justified if it succeeds in checking the greater dangers of excessive autonomy and the dilution or distortion of the public's credit without its consent.*

---

*Comment: Mr. Robinson takes exception to the Task Force recommendations on industrial revenue bonds, pollution control bonds, and tax-exempt entities.

The U.S. Supreme Court held in *Pollock v. Farmers' Loan & Trust Company*, 157 U.S. 429 (1895) *rev'd on rehearing* 158 U.S. 601 (1895), that a federal tax on interest on bonds of states and political subdivisions was unconstitutional as a violation of the reciprocal immunity doctrine. Some commentators claim that the Sixteenth Amendment, which became effective in 1913, repudiated the rule of the *Pollock* case. But the cases decided by the Supreme Court under the Sixteenth Amendment, the legislative history of the amendment in Congress during the period when it was being ratified by the state legislatures, as well as subsequent construction by Congress demonstrate that such claims are unsupported by any judicial precedent. Thus, Mr. Robinson believes that from a constitutional point of view, the Task Force's recommendations are of doubtful legal validity.

The Task Force urges the enactment of legislation to remove the potential for abuse in municipal bond advanced refunding.

Advanced refundings are municipal bonds sold to refinance existing debt before the outstanding debt matures or is otherwise eligible for redemption. Refundings in general become attractive when interest levels drop and loans can be refinanced at a lower rate of interest. Tax-exempt borrowers also can use the proceeds of the tax-exempt refunding to invest in higher yielding taxable securities. Thus, advanced refunding carries a powerful potential for profits, giving the issuer a "riskless" profit on the differential between the two rates of interest.

By the mid-1960s, advanced refunding had gotten out of hand and was swelling the supply of tax-exempt securities to the detriment of the market. Although subsequent legislation and regulations eliminated much of the interest-savings advantages of advanced refundings for issuers, they had the unfortunate effect of shifting much of the profits from the

In addition, as one policy consideration, he feels that deference should be given to state legislative actions which determine that the financing authorized by such legislatures serves a public purpose. These legislative findings have, in many cases, been sustained by the highest courts of the respective states. In addition, the U.S. Supreme Court has sustained the state court findings that such financing constitutes a public purpose.

As an additional policy consideration, he points to the futility of legislative or regulatory attempts to limit the exemption of interest on state and local borrowing. The amendments to Section 103(c) of the Internal Revenue Code of 1954 set forth in the Revenue and Expenditure Control Act of 1968 and the amendments to Section 103(d) of the code set forth in the Tax Reform Act of 1969 have proved unsuccessful because they present almost insurmountable problems of interpretation and enforcement. Both amendments have been the subject of numerous temporary, proposed, and permanent regulations which are, for the most part, unworkable.

He believes that misuse of the tax exemption is a major concern. However, the proposals presented by the Task Force cause him even more concern. He believes that state and local governments should be more concerned about the evils than they have been. The proposed solution should involve action at the state level rather than affect the basic tax exemption of state and local governmental obligations. He fully agrees with the Task Force that the tax treatment of users should be studied and depreciation benefits eliminated where tax-exempt financing is available.

Mr. Niebling wishes to join with Mr. Robinson in that portion of his comment expressing support for greater concern by state and local governments about such possible misuses and also recommends that the basic solution should be at the state level.

issuer to those who underwrite the refunding issue and manage the investment of the proceeds. Thus, the reform has given the middleman an incentive to promote advanced refundings. The profits earned by underwriters at the time of the bond sale and investment of proceeds can equal, and sometimes exceed, the discounted interest savings available to issuers.

Certain advanced refundings are justified for purposes of reducing interest costs in the distant future. *But the Task Force recommends that the government should require the proceeds of advance refunding issues to be invested in special Treasury obligations.* Such obligations should be readily available. Borrowers should not be permitted the additional advantage of increasing at will the supply of tax-exempts and playing the arbitrage game at the expense of other tax-exempt issuers or the federal taxpayer.*

*Comment: Mr. Robinson considers the past history of legislative attempts to limit advance refunding to be a good example of the futility of dealing with the problem by federal legislation. In 1966, the Treasury announced that it would no longer issue tax rulings in certain advance refunding transactions and that it would study the problems presented and report on its results. No study was ever conducted, but the Tax Reform Act of 1969 eliminated the tax exemption for interest on arbitrage bonds. The Treasury labored hard over regulations for several years but was unable to set forth any guidelines that are meaningful. In fact, advance refunding, both good and bad, has reached historic proportions.

He recommends the deletion of Section 103(d) from the code and the issuance of a statement by the Treasury similar in nature to that contained in the Treasury announcement of 1966. Such action would appear to limit the abuses of arbitrage bonds.

Mr. Niebling endorses this view.

MORE ASSISTANCE BY THE STATES

The Task Force urges state governments to take a more active role in providing technical assistance and services to improve the debt management of local governments.

With some notable exceptions, past state actions in this sphere have focused on constraining local governmental debt management through laws and other regulations that limit the type, amount, or uses of debt. The Task Force recommends a more positive approach, reiterating the finding of the original Twentieth Century Fund Task Force on Municipal Bond Credit Ratings, namely, that the states should provide technical assistance to local governments in their debt issuance and management activities.

Most local governmental units enter the bond market only infrequently and for relatively small amounts of funds. When they do so, they must compete for money with larger state and local governments and their agencies that make regular use of this market. In this competition, the smaller and relatively unknown borrower often comes out second best. Smaller issuers incur proportionately higher costs in marketing debt, they often lack sophistication in design and marketing, and their securities receive fewer bids. Most of these issuers must depend upon local sources for funds; national market interest is sparse and can be exceedingly expensive to attract.

State assistance and involvement can take several forms, and the specific services that could be offered profitably depend upon local circumstances. A state department or agency should make available to all local governments professional staff counsel and advice on the technical requirements of designing and marketing new issues. In particular, a centralized agency at the state level can provide an effective and economical solution to the market's needs for more timely, complete, and standardized credit information. Although some larger units do not need the assistance of such a state agency, most small jurisdictions cannot afford to retain the professional staff necessary to manage only occasional needs for financing.

State Detection and Supervision of Financially Troubled Local Governments

The Task Force recommends that state governments institute procedures for the early detection of financial difficulties in their local units and that they provide a mechanism for assisting and—if necessary—controlling the finances of governments that fall into fiscal crisis.

The financial crisis in New York State resulting from the overextension of New York City, major state agencies, and a few smaller jurisdictions clearly illustrates the epidemic qualities of financial stress. If local emergencies are to be prevented or at least isolated rapidly and cured, a mechanism must be in place to spot difficulties at an early stage and take steps to avert a crisis. A strong financial-reporting system that gives a clear and rapid picture of the fiscal conditions of governments can provide early warnings of such difficulties. The collection and analysis of such reports is not enough; monitoring must be bolstered by strong educational and technical assistance programs aggressively promoted by state officials.

In those cases in which persuasion and voluntary assistance are insufficient to stave off default, the state should be prepared to step in and maintain direct supervision of the government's finances until it has recovered the ability to function independently. Such standby powers, and the willingness to exercise them, will help prevent disasters. The prospect of such state action in emergencies should be reassuring to investors and help to keep the credit markets available to borrowers even in times of stress.

Consolidation of Local Government Borrowing through State Bond Banks*

On the basis of successful applications of the bond-bank technique, the Task Force believes that states should make more serious efforts to consolidate the borrowings of smaller local governments. State-sponsored agencies to consolidate the borrowing of smaller units, which are frequently unrated and financially unsophisticated, may help to lower the cost of borrowing for local governments. The bond-bank device, pioneered in Vermont and Maine, permits the voluntary pooling of many small obligations into larger, more efficient borrowings. In these states, such combined borrowings have produced economies of scale in the costs of preparing issues for market, attracted more bidders, and reduced the risks of holding the debt of small issuers. Properly designed, a bond bank can secure better market acceptance and lower rates than those available to small, infrequent bond issuers.

Bond banks operate on a voluntary basis. In theory, such banks might coerce local governmental units into participating or exclude them or engage in favoritism. But the Task Force has found no evidence of such problems in the bond banks that are in operation. In Maine and Vermont, not all units have chosen to participate, but those that have, have benefited. Cost reductions stem from a variety of sources: lower legal, printing, and advisory fees; reduced underwriting spreads; and lower reoffering yields. The lower borrowing costs, generated largely by the presence of superior ratings, have resulted in the most significant savings—some 40 to 50 basis points—in consolidated borrowings. The cost of the consolidated issue is lower than that of an individual borrowing by 3 to 5 percent of the principal amount of the borrowing.

*Comment: Mr. Niebling believes that additional "security" beyond that of individual municipalities is necessary in order for the bond bank to obtain a better rating and lower interest costs. Otherwise the bond bank will sell at the level of the lowest credit involved. Such additional security is available through the establishment of a debt service reserve to be used in case of default by member municipalities, a state guarantee, or a moral obligation pledge.

Mr. Leone endorses this view.

SPECIAL POLICIES FOR FISCAL EMERGENCIES

Emergency Credit Assistance

The Task Force believes that the federal government should contemplate the possible necessity of future emergency relief to certain large state and local borrowers in need of temporary credit assistance to avoid default. However, such assistance should be provided only in those few instances in which the consequences of default would be of major national impact. A condition of such credit assistance should be adoption of a plan to remedy the fiscal imbalance. Furthermore, the federal government, while properly taking every precaution to protect its loan, should examine the underlying causes of the problem and should take steps to correct those conditions caused by inequities in handling its own programs—such as welfare and health—at the local level.

The Task Force does not believe that emergency federal credit assistance should become a crutch to be relied upon or that it can substitute for more basic solutions, including the institution of new or reformed federal assistance programs. On the other hand, financial disasters—whether self-inflicted or caused by circumstances beyond the immediate control of the debtor—can do lasting damage, far outweighing any benefits from teaching a lesson to creditors and debtors.

While discipline must be maintained in these situations, it seems best to do an orderly job—which may well require temporary infusions of cash. In those few cases in which such help is necessary, the credit assistance extended must be under such terms and conditions that it hastens recovery and discourages its use. Because the causes and conditions will vary from case to case, the Task Force does not believe such assistance should be provided without a thorough congressional review. Furthermore, it recommends that where credit assistance is given, it be in the form of a direct loan from the Treasury to assure that it is given in the most cost-efficient ways, the creditor position of the federal government is clear, and the transaction has maximum visibility in the budget.*

Direct Allocation of Credit

The Task Force generally opposes those proposals that rely upon direct credit controls or mandated investments as methods of allocating credit among competing users and uses.

The understandable pressures upon various groups to strive for competitive advantage in obtaining capital funds have fostered a variety of proposals to interject new, non-market allocative mechanisms into the capital-raising process. The Task Force opposes large-scale adoption of such proposals, however well-intentioned they may be, because of the potentially disruptive and distorted effects they may have on the entire capital market.

Under certain proposals, the amount and composition of municipal securities held by financial institutions would be largely determined by legislative fiat. At the extreme, some states have introduced proposals that would require institutions to earmark part of their assets for specific amounts and types of municipal securities. Legislatively mandating investments in this manner raises a number of serious questions. Rechanneling financial flows to assist a narrow class of beneficiaries raises the questions of what sectors of the market will lose on the exchange and at what cost. As a practical matter, enforcing such allocative schemes would be difficult without a substantial regulatory mechanism and its attendant costs. Moreover, substituting political decisions for management decisions might seriously erode investor and depositor confidence.†

---

*Comment: Mr. Garrett does not agree that federal emergency assistance should be left to specific congressional action in each case. He recommends that Congress establish the governing principles and authority under which the Executive Branch, presumably Treasury, can act in appropriate cases.

†*Comment:* Mr. Garrett would emphasize the inequities and social dangers of any legal compulsion or extralegal pressure for pension funds of any sort, including those of state or municipal employees or their unions, to invest in the bonds of local governmental units.

Messrs. Hoff and Robinson endorse this view.

Another class of proposals—a special federal bank, frequently called "Urbank," to make direct loans to state and local governments, a federal agency to conduct secondary market operations, or programs to provide direct and general federal guarantees of municipal debt—would interpose the federal government between borrowers and lenders. These proposals would substitute federal debt for state and local government debt. In turn, the scrutiny of a private market would be replaced by a system of administrative controls and rationing schemes to determine lending terms and eligibility standards. It would be unlikely that this process would duplicate the discipline exercised by the private market. Such a system is also potentially discriminatory: issuers who have carefully managed their finances would be treated the same as those that were less disciplined or even profligate. Furthermore, even the most carefully designed and administered operation runs the risk of political interference. The Task Force feels that the goals underlying such mechanisms can be more effectively met through changes that would enhance the operation of the private market.

While it may be necessary, and even appropriate, for the federal government to serve as a lender of last resort to prevent massive dislocations in the event of municipal bankruptcies, the Task Force believes, as has been noted, that such emergency assistance should be provided only on a case-by-case basis and never as a convenient escape hatch from financial difficulties.*

Proposals Regarding the Federal Reserve

Various proposals for using Federal Reserve System mechanisms to strengthen and stabilize the market for municipal

---

Comment: Messrs. Pechman, Hoff, and Yarborough do not believe that present market arrangements, even when modified to the extent proposed in this Report, are certain to provide ample credit facilities for urgently needed state-local borrowing. Under the circumstances, they cannot agree that a federal credit facility or federal guarantees for municipal debt should be forever excluded from consideration.

securities have been made. One such proposal involves the use of special "reserve credits" to stimulate the demand for municipal bonds. These credits would permit commercial banks or other financial institutions to reduce their legal reserve requirements by offsetting such nonearning assets with municipal securities. Although a reserve credit would act as a short-run stimulus to the municipal market when first implemented, over the longer run, the adjustments of portfolios would not produce any permanent net increases in holdings of municipals. Furthermore, opening the Federal Reserve window to municipal bonds would inevitably lead to demands for similar treatment of mortgages or other financial instruments.

Proposals for legislation that would enable the Federal Reserve to carry out open-market transactions in municipal securities are felt to be equally objectionable. The principal responsibility of the Federal Reserve is to develop and implement monetary policy, and open-market transactions are the principal tools for carrying out this mission. The federal securities markets are used for this purpose primarily because they can absorb monetary policy transactions with minimal disturbances to price and yield relationships. Involvement in less resilient markets would require the Federal Reserve to divert its attention from the difficult task of achieving overall monetary goals to the technical task of maintaining internal market stability. It would expose the operations of the Federal Reserve to political pressure, particularly in the selection of the municipal securities it chooses to deal in.

DISCLOSURE OF INFORMATION

The recent credit problems of some major borrowers in the municipal bond market have focused attention on the very real need for full disclosure of information by borrowers. The Task Force believes that greater uniformity is needed in the information provided for municipal securities transactions and that national standards for financial disclosure should be established. The economic and political ramifications of direct regulation in this area of the capital markets are of such far-reaching importance that any action should be approached with caution and only after a thorough examination of the various choices. The Task Force therefore supports voluntary efforts of all market participants to create such standards. Even if such efforts prove insufficient, they will help in the formulation of possible future mandatory systems.

There are two views of how full disclosure can best be achieved. In one view, adequate disclosure can be developed by market forces outside the purview of direct federal regulation. The public nature of the issuers and the superior risk record of municipal securities, it is argued, ensure the development of standards flexible enough to meet the variety of the market but thorough enough to satisfy the needs of investors. Development of higher standards will be hastened because of the existing liabilities under the antifraud statutes and the natural functioning of market participants to minimize the risk of fraud by exercising care in the information provided to the market. This view has the support of issuers who are hesitant to turn the regulation of information over to a federal authority for fear that such regulation may become increasingly restrictive and onerous and may well undermine the autonomy of state and local borrowers.

The other view points to the regulatory powers of the federal government establishing national standards for disclosure in securities transactions. State and local governmental issuers historically have been beyond the scope of direct federal securities regulation; it is argued, however, that the recent action applying regulation to municipal securities dealers and other changes in the market imposes at least some form of direct control over issuing governments.

Moreover, the current uncertainty about the liabilities of various participants—including issuers—under the antifraud provisions may bring chaotic conditions and may result in a de facto system of disclosure brought on by disparate and perhaps conflicting court decisions and enforcement actions by the Securities and Exchange Commission. Those who take this point of view maintain that even if the market could voluntarily develop a fair and effective standard, the realities of judicial and regulatory action would eventually force federal legislation and perhaps would do so under more unfavorable conditions.

In balancing the two arguments, the Task Force concludes that legislative caution in this area is essential.* Both history and reason demonstrate that municipal securities are different from other capital market obligations and must be treated as such in the securities laws. Because these offerings are so numerous and diverse, regulations that are too restrictive or cumbersome could cause unnecessary expense and delay. Nor should the possibilities of political interference be dismissed lightly. Despite the obvious difficulties of New York City and

---

Comment: Messrs. Hoff and Pechman are concerned that the use of the term "legislative caution" in this context might be construed by some readers to be a recommendation for further delay and inaction on the part of Congress. Recent events have amply demonstrated that federal legislation to provide national standards for municipal securities disclosure is urgently needed. Of course, the legislation should be drafted carefully and with due consideration to the question of liability noted in the next paragraph.

Mr. Garrett favors early enactment of federal disclosure legislation as presently embodied in the Municipal Securities Full Disclosure Act of 1976 (S. 2969)—which empowers the Securities and Exchange Commission to establish disclosure standards, does not require preoffering SEC review, and grants exemptions based on small size with further provisions relating to the liabilities of the several parties.

Mr. Smeal does not concur fully in this conclusion of the Task Force. Although he concurs in the view that a considerable amount of care must be exercised in the development of particular disclosure standards and in the resolution of underwriter and issuer liability questions, he doubts that a voluntary framework will be adequate to achieve this result. Therefore, he is in favor of mandatory disclosure and uniform disclosure standards on a national basis.

He also believes that liability consequences and limitations for issuers and underwriters should be addressed in such federal legislation. In his view, such legislation should emphasize the provision of annual reports by issuers, with the objective of reducing disclosure burdens with respect to particular issues of reporting entities. He believes that the possibility should be explored of appointing a national council, composed exclusively of state and local officials, pursuant to such legislation to promulgate the appropriate disclosure standards for particular types of issuers and issues.

other major borrowers, it is not clear that investors have suffered large-scale abuse or that in those cases where they have, they do not already have sufficient remedies.

Furthermore, were a national standard for municipal securities disclosure to be devised, it is clear that the question of liability for the provision of the information would have to be resolved as well. Otherwise the major causes of uncertainty would remain or perhaps be exacerbated.

The Task Force does unite to urge market participants to work voluntarily for improved municipal disclosure and to cooperate to resolve many of the difficult substantive and procedural problems surrounding disclosure. Without federal legislation, these efforts will be necessary if lasting improvements in informing the market are to be made. With federal legislation, such experience will help make any mandated system more responsive to the distinctive needs of the municipal bond market investor and issuer.

The Task Force reaffirms the earlier recommendation by the Twentieth Century Fund Task Force on Municipal Bond Credit Ratings that a national data-gathering service—a data bank—be created to compile and analyze information about state and local governments and their securities. The bank would offer many services, but one of its major objectives would be to develop and implement standard reporting formats and to encourage the timely retrieval and dissemination of such information to the market. Such a central source of information would provide a better basis for credit analysis and stimulate improvements in analytical techniques.

The details of the organization, sponsorship, and financing of a data bank need to be explored. But it has become increasingly clear that such a service is needed.

Background Paper

by Ronald W. Forbes and John E. Petersen

PREFACE

The market for state and local government securities is one of the nation's most remarkable institutions. Peculiarly American, with roots embedded deeply in the economic and political traditions of the country, the municipal bond market has many distinguishing features, foremost of which is the exemption of its interest income from federal income taxes.

But that is not the reason the market exists. It performs the vital economic and political function of raising private capital to meet the needs of a large, diverse, and far-flung branch of our federal system—the state and local governments. The mission and methods of those governments fluctuate in response to changes in the perceptions, aspirations, and wealth of the society. And the municipal bond market, in which governments strike bargains with investors and exchange promises for the loan of resources, also moves in sympathy with these changes.

The market is not without its problems, as both this paper and the accompanying report of the Task Force reveal. Our assignment has been to examine the structure and operation of the market and to suggest how these might be improved. We have looked at a large variety of suggestions for reform, stretching from relatively minor tinkering with tax codes and the design of debt instruments to the creation of alternative capital-raising mechanisms. Our aim has been to be objective and comprehensive. The views represented in this background paper are solely those of the authors. If we have a caveat, it is that the eye focused on flaws in the present market not lose sight of its strengths and accomplishments.

Many have helped us in this project. We wish to thank Mary Petersen and Carl Reiser, Judith Jacobson, and Beverly Goldberg of the Twentieth Century Fund, who at various stages edited the manuscript and improved it. The members of the Task Force were most helpful in their comments on the draft and their close examination of the issues, which were both instructive and inspiring to us. We are particularly grateful to Walter Klein, a fellow economist, who with wit and charity not only helped us to sharpen the tools of our trade but also to make their products more readable.

But the greatest expression of appreciation and the dedication must be reserved for our wives, Jean and Mary, who in every way shared in this venture. They confirm our notion that certain fixed commitments into which we entered a few years ago continue to yield returns beyond measure.

Ronald W. Forbes   John E. Petersen
Albany, New York   Fairfax, Virginia

1

Introduction

The summer of 1975 brought the curtain down dramatically on a remarkable 15-year era of growth, change, and innovation in the municipal bond market. In July, in a last-ditch effort to contain the New York City credit crisis, the Municipal Assistance Corporation (MAC) began an attempt to sell $3 billion in bonds in three months. Only the federal government had ever attempted such a feat. Indeed, the $1 billion worth of bonds sold by MAC was more than double the size of the largest bond issue ever sold in the private market. But the scheme failed, and the municipal bond market continues to feel the shock waves of that event.

The era of growth that had just ended passed through two phases. In the first stage, lasting throughout most of the 1960s, the municipal market often performed like a prodigy. The volume of state and local governmental borrowing, starting at an annual rate of $11.5 billion, more than trebled in 10 years to reach a volume of some $35.0 billion in 1970. The rapidly expanding market for municipals helped states and communities fulfill many of their important capital needs in areas such as education, water and sewage systems, and highways.

The steady upward surge was slowed by the periodic credit crunches of 1966 and 1969, when a scarcity of capital and high interest rates particularly affected the market for municipal securities. But tax-exempt sales recovered and made up for lost ground. Then, in 1974, recession compounded the problems of inflation. In 1974–75, interest rates on municipal long-term bonds and short-term notes matched or exceeded the record high levels of 1970. The stage was set for a debacle—and it happened in New York.

The conditions leading to such a confrontation—somewhere—were building during the early 1970s. State governments, municipalities, public authorities, and quasi-governmental agencies were pushing the use of tax-exempt bonds and notes into new—and sometimes questionable—territory. Some of this activity resulted from the relaxation by the IRS of its restrictions on the use of tax-exempt issues to assist private enterprise in meeting public demands for pollution control, housing, and public amenities such as stadiums. For these and other purposes, various devices were employed, among them indirect guarantees and leasehold arrangements. Short-term borrowing, particularly in connection with the postponement of long-term debt, became an increasingly significant factor in the tax-exempt market.

Many of these situations proved hazardous as inflation drove up governmental costs that could not be passed along to taxpayers and as receipts failed to rise or actually fell off. As the economic troubles of 1974 deepened, a number of shaky situations began coming apart—particularly in the older metropolitan areas that had long been in difficulty.

PALL OVER THE MARKETPLACE

Throughout 1975, the market was rocked by uncertainties about its two largest borrowers, New York City and New York State. With an approximately $25 billion debt in question, the scene of action shifted from New York State and its hasty shuffling of funds to keep an army of creditors at bay to the court of last resort, the federal government.

No one who read the newspapers, watched television, or spoke to neighbors could miss the issue. National polls were taken; presidential addresses were given; ideologies and reputations were pitted against one another. Meanwhile, in Congress, the issue of how to punish the guilty and protect the innocent was debated at length, while the fate of New York City and the municipal bond market hung in the balance.

For more than three decades, many investors in municipal bonds had routinely and trustingly invested their own and other people's money in what they perceived to be lackluster but strong securities. Their faith shaken for the first time since the Depression, they withheld new funds and began to ask questions about both the promises to pay and the debtors who issued the paper promises. Some creditors sued the city of New York to recoup their losses, and the Securities and Exchange Commission began to take an interest in municipal affairs. The passage of municipal bankruptcy legislation by Congress only increased the financial community's questioning mood.

The possibility of default has cast a pall over the marketplace: investors are demanding greater premiums from borrowers who are thought to have payment difficulties, and certain borrowers are finding it difficult to obtain any financing. The New York crisis has received most of the attention, but a ripple of worry has been felt throughout the market. Rates on lower-investment-grade municipal bonds (Baa) increased in 1975 and have stayed at the wide margin of more than 1 percentage point, or nearly 20 percent, more than rates on high-quality bonds (Aaa). Spreads of this magnitude have not been seen in the municipal market since the early 1960s.

Despite these difficulties, the municipal bond market achieved a record level of new borrowing (estimated at about $60 billion in 1975). However, the continued high cost of borrowing derailed some planned projects and forced borrowers to raise future taxes and user charges to meet debt service payments—a situation that still holds for some borrowers in mid-1976 even though there has been a remarkable decline in interest rates generally.

THREE LEVELS OF STRUCTURAL PROBLEMS

The turmoil of the past several years has disclosed structural problems that have very serious implications for this vitally important financial sector. State and local governments must rely upon continued use of credit markets for long-term financing of capital facilities and for short-term financing of cash needs to bridge the cycles of income and outlay. But recent events have once again demonstrated how highly vulnerable the municipal market is to fluctuations in economic activity and financial flows. These fluctuations greatly affect the cost and availability of credit to governments.

What, then, must be done? The present turmoil in the marketplace arises from a tangle of causes that admit no single, simple solution. Nevertheless, it is possible to separate the capital market problems of state and local governments into three broad areas of concern.

One area of difficulty faced by borrowers relates to technical or marketing difficulties. These are created by the unique characteristics of the tax-exempt security and the resulting complexity of the distribution system. The market is inundated by a vast number of individually tailored issues of securities, creating an inefficient market.

As a consequence, the reception given governmental borrowers by the credit markets is uneven. Through the years, strong and significant variations have persisted in the cost and availability of credit. Such variations are related to the size, purpose, and location of governmental borrowers. They can and do reflect certain real differences in risk and cost, but they are also often the result of market eccentricities and insularities. These defects impede the efficient allocation of nationwide resources among public units. Within the limits of supply and demand, participants must now face the problem of making this market operate more efficiently.

A second area of difficulty relates to the underlying supply and demand characteristic of the municipal market. This is a fundamental issue involving the long-term adequacy of investor demand for tax-exempt securities and the periodic imbalances of demand and supply.

One of the most dismaying consequences of the turmoil in the financial markets has been the resulting fluctuations in borrowing costs for state and local governments. These changes have been sharp and steep, displaying a far greater volatility than that of most other credit markets. Gyrations in the cost of credit add another element of uncertainty to municipal budgets and cash flows. They are already squeezed in a vise between inflation, with its erosion of purchasing power, and recession, with its stultifying effect on revenues and its increasing demands on expenditures.

A major reason for the volatility of borrowing costs in the municipal market is the unique reliance of the market for tax-exempt securities on the investment preferences of these groups: commercial banks, property and casualty insurance companies, and individuals. Cyclical changes and long-term shifts in the preferences of any one of these sectors can cause—indeed, most emphatically, have caused—peculiarly drastic effects on the terms and conditions of borrowing faced by state and local governments.

This situation calls into serious question the efficiency of tax exemption when viewed as a form of subsidy to lower the cost of borrowing. The reduced effectiveness of tax exemption is demonstrated by a rising ratio of tax-exempt to taxable interest rates. In 1975, the interest rates of Aaa-rated municipal bonds averaged 73 percent of those of like-rated corporate bonds. For investors with a marginal income tax rate of 48 percent (the maximum corporate tax rate), this indicates that tax-free returns were about 40 percent higher than that available, after taxes, on a fully taxable corporate security.

All of this, together with other problems raised by the market's exclusive reliance on tax exemption as a means of subsidy, opens wide the question of whether or not alternative means of support for public projects should be explored.

A third area of difficulty concerns the competition between the public and private sectors for those funds that are available for investment. Decisions to improve the flow of capital of the state and local sectors ultimately depend on fundamental choices about the allocation of resources, both between public and private enterprise and within the public sector.

By mid-1975, it had become clear that states and localities could no longer be free to share their market with others and still expect to enjoy the maximum benefit of tax-exempt borrowing themselves. As long as tax-exempt rates provide some savings, state and local agencies will continue to seek financing, even at the cost of pushing up rates for other governmental borrowers. Such behavior generally lessens the efficiency of tax exemption. It may therefore be desirable to restrain some forms of tax-exempt financing in order to facilitate municipal financing for other needs with a higher social priority.

FRAMEWORK FOR JUDGING PROPOSALS

A lengthy list of suggested remedies for these problems has been actively debated. The debate reflects different theories regarding the causes of high interest rates and the uneven flow of credit to state and local borrowers. But the debate obviously has been conditioned by the special interests of the different participants in the market. Resolution of these issues is difficult because of the lack of both data and empirical studies of the implications of suggested policies. This, of course, is a common complaint about policy analysis in any area: the growing complexity of problems often outstrips the methodology.

Specific proposals for changing the operation and structure of municipal borrowing are examined in this background paper in terms of their effectiveness, efficiency, and equity. Effectiveness, in this context, is the degree to which a policy will alter the cost and availability of borrowing faced by state and local governmental units. Efficiency of alternative policies is the relationship between the overall costs of direct or indirect subsidies of interest rates and the benefits accruing to intended beneficiaries of the policies. Equity is judged in terms of how a policy affects the social objectives inherent in a system of progressive taxation.

Proposals also must be judged in terms of their feasibility. A proposal is considered feasible if it is politically acceptable, is practicable, and has a reasonable chance of being implemented. The authors have been guided by these criteria in examining the structural conditions of supply and demand in the market and the various proposals for improving the market that have been suggested.

2

A Primer on Municipal Securities

The distinguishing feature of the municipal security is its tax-exempt status. Interest income earned by investors who purchase these securities is not subject to federal or, frequently, to various state and local income taxes. Since tax exemption permits state and local governments to borrow at lower rates of interest, their securities are different from those of other borrowers, including the federal government and private corporations. Municipal securities have a special market composed of individual or institutional investors seeking non-taxable income.

Municipal securities are debt obligations having fixed maturities and fixed rates of interest. But they are backed by many different kinds of security in terms of the resources that the governments pledge to meet the payments of principal and interest, or debt service charges. Municipal securities conventionally are divided into two broad categories: (1) general obligations secured by the full faith and credit—the taxing power—of a government and (2) revenue or special-fund obligations secured on the revenues or receipts of a project or special fund rather than by the full taxing power of a borrower.

Most governmental securities are debentures. They are secured on the general creditworthiness of the borrower's promises, not on the real or financial assets to which the borrower has rights of possession in the case of default. Bond-holders cannot be paid off with fire hydrants or classrooms if their municipal debtor defaults. Great emphasis therefore is placed on the flow of revenues and the ability of the investor to get a first claim on them.

State and local governmental issuers, the uses of proceeds, and the controlling legislation under which governments undertake capital projects and market securities are extremely diverse. The result is an almost infinite variety in the characteristics of the securities that are offered.

BONDS AND NOTES

Like all credit-market instruments, municipal securities are classified by the period of debt the issuer incurs. Usually the term of a municipal security is closely aligned with the type of activity it finances.

"Bonds" are long-term obligations, maturing in not less than one year. Sold primarily to finance long-term capital investments, bonds have traditionally comprised the bulk of state and local governmental financing, although this pattern has altered over the past decade.

"Notes" are short-term obligations with a maximum maturity of one year or less. Notes are customarily used to smooth out the differences in cash flow between revenues and expenditures, to meet unexpected deficits, or to provide interim financing of projects in anticipation of later bond sales. State laws and market preferences have traditionally attempted to restrict short-term borrowing to "working-capital" needs and to reserve long-term borrowing for long-lived capital projects.

But there are exceptions. For example, notes issued in anticipation of revenues or the proceeds of bond sales may be renewed or "rolled over" for several years and thus provide a long-term source of debt capital. Less frequently, bonds may be sold to pay off an accumulation of past operating deficits or to meet some other financial emergency.

Municipal bonds differ in their maturity structure—that is, in the way the borrowed principal is repaid. Only a few municipals are sold with a single rate of interest and a single maturity applying to all the bonds in the issue. Most bonds are sold in serial form, each series having its own date of maturity; this means that installments of the principal must be paid to certain holders each year. Thus, a municipal bond issue actually consists of a bundle of issues, each carrying its own coupon, amount, and maturity. Typically, municipal bond certificates are issued in denominations of $5,000. Most new bond issues run 15 to 25 years to final maturity, although maturities stretching to 30 or 40 years are not uncommon.

There are two forms of municipal bond certificates: bearer bonds and registered bonds. Bearer bonds are more common than registered bonds in the municipal market; the reverse is true in the corporate securities market. Bearer bonds can be transferred among investors without notification to the issuer and therefore allow the investor to remain anonymous, but they are bulky and expensive to ship and process and require security measures for safekeeping.

The number of different types of securities and the serial nature of the bonds, combined with the large number of issues, make the bidding, reoffering, and trading of municipal securities highly complex. The municipal bond market is an extremely heterogeneous one.

UNDERWRITING AND TRADING

Most new municipal bond issues are "underwritten," that is, purchased by a bond dealer or a group of dealers from the issuer and then distributed to investors. Most states require municipal general-obligation bonds to be sold at a public competitive bidding, and many revenue-bond issues are sold in the same way. Negotiated sale, the usual method of selling corporate securities, is seldom used in marketing general obligations, but it accounts for about half of all sales of revenue bonds. Private placement of any municipal issue is extremely rare. Underwriters, who may be small regional-securities dealers, Wall Street investment bankers, or giant money-market banks, act as risk-bearing middlemen. They purchase the bonds from the issuers, and they attempt to distribute or reoffer the securities to investors. The difference between the price paid the issuer and the price received from the investor (the so-called reoffering price) constitutes the underwriter's compensation. In the municipal market, this spread or gross profit typically runs about $10 to $20 per $1,000 bond—but the hoped-for profit can be turned into a loss if the market reverses or if demand is misjudged.

Because financing the underwriting of a bond issue involves a heavy capital commitment, dealers usually seek partners and form syndicates. When the syndicate that will offer the bonds is chosen through competitive bidding, its reoffering prices are usually set according to a scale of interest rates decided upon prior to the competitive bidding. In some cases, the reoffering rates may have to be altered, depending on how well the bidding has gone and on changes in market conditions. Approximately 30 days after the bonds have been awarded to the winning syndicate, they are delivered and payment takes place.

Although approximately 450 securities dealers and banks underwrite municipal bonds, some 100 firms dominate the field. They account for more than 90 percent of the dollar volume of underwriting, and the 10 largest banks and dealers account for 40 to 50 percent of all bonds underwritten.

The secondary or trading market for municipal bonds is made up of approximately 800 dealers and banks throughout the country. They trade outstanding securities in order to provide liquidity for investor holdings. Municipal bonds, unlike corporate securities, are traded exclusively over the counter and are not listed on any organized exchange. There is no regularly published information about the size of the municipal secondary market, but estimates indicate that the secondary market has been approximately one to two times the size of the new-issue market.

THE MARKET FOR MUNICIPALS

Governmental borrowers compete for funds in the private capital market, where prospective investors weigh the relative risks of and returns on a host of alternative financial instruments and on "real" capital such as land and condominiums. The tax-exemption feature, the main attraction of municipal bonds, makes for complex investment decisions: one individual may weigh complicated tax considerations against other personal or institutional goals and restraints; a rural banker may want to support his community by purchasing tax-anticipation notes below the going market rate of interest; an individual may regularly purchase tax-exempt bonds to build up a stable retirement income; and an urban banker may manage a multi-billion-dollar portfolio and trade securities on the basis of small changes in market price.

The demand for municipals is concentrated almost entirely in three investor groups with high marginal tax rates: commercial banks, property and casualty insurance companies, and "households." This third category mainly comprises individual investors and personal trusts. At the end of 1974, these three groups held almost all (95 percent) of the outstanding municipal securities. Although the municipal bond market is widely believed to be the preserve of the rich individual investor, the most important buyer in this market (as in other securities markets) increasingly is the rich institution.

While state and local governments as a group are heavily dependent upon the three major buyers of their credit, this dependence is not mutual: municipals are not the preferred choice for investment by any of the three groups. In fact, their combined holdings of municipal securities at the end of 1975 came to less than 6.5 percent of their total financial assets. Because tax-exempt securities have a special and limited market, inviting instability, the tax-exempt feature is indeed a mixed blessing—a fact that is becoming increasingly evident.

3

The Market of the 1960s and 1970s: Growth and Expediency

State and local governmental borrowing has grown rapidly over the past quarter of a century. The overall volume of annual sales has risen from a level of $5.3 billion in 1950 to $60 billion in 1975 and has been split about evenly between long-term bonds and short-term notes. The dollar volume of new bond sales has typically equaled 50 percent or more of total capital outlays made by the nonfederal public sector. The annual volume of short-term borrowing implies that notes are the means of financing about 15 percent of state and local expenditures at one time or another.

Total debt outstanding was an estimated $225 billion in 1975, about 90 percent of which was long-term. Because some of the old debt is repaid each year, the net cash gain from new borrowing is therefore less than the gross sales of bonds and notes. Long-term debt retirements, paid from current revenues or occasionally by additional borrowing, and interest comprise the annual burden of debt on current receipts. In 1974, the total debt service was $17 billion—$9 billion in long-term debt repayment and $8 billion interest on all debt, both short- and long-term. This debt service equaled approximately 10 percent of the $165 billion state and local governments raised from their own sources in that year.[1]

The increase in note sales, begun during the credit crunch of 1969 and 1970, went from $9 billion in 1969 to nearly $30 billion in 1974 and 1975. State and local governments increased their use of short-term credit for various reasons.

First, faced with the steep rise in long-term rates, many long-term borrowers while waiting for better market conditions wanted to postpone definitive financing without interrupting spending plans. Second, the volume of short-term borrowing was enlarged steadily by federally backed public housing and urban renewal notes, which grew from $4.9 billion in sales in 1968 to $10.5 billion by 1974.[2] But the events of 1975 were to prove that the buildup of short-term debt was not without its costs.

If one figures in short-term debt as a potential cash claim, then annual short- and long-term retirements and interest payments amount to about $35 billion. This so-called full debt service represents more than 20 percent of the total revenues now raised annually by state and local governments from taxes and user charges.

At the end of 1975, state and local debt outstanding equaled 7.5 percent of the $3 trillion in net public and private debt held by the public. State and local obligations are thus important to the total debt structure in the economy. The volume of these securities has grown somewhat faster than the volume of all other capital-market instruments; yet the sector's relative position in the aggregate of debt claims has changed only slightly—from 18 percent of all nonfederal credit-market debt outstanding in 1950 to 18.5 percent in 1974.

THE DRAMATIC INCREASE IN REVENUE BONDS

During the past 15 years, the dramatic growth in overall volume and the shift toward short-term debt were by no means the only major trends in the municipal bond market. Equally significant have been the profound changes in the composition of the different sectors of the market in terms of the security used to back the bonds, the purposes for which they are issued, and the types of borrowers. Thanks to the ingenuity of legal counsel, underwriters, and government officials, many novel tax-exempt financing devices have flourished in the last few years. Among these are the advanced refunding of outstanding debt; tax-increment bonds; and other expedients designed to circumvent debt ceilings, voter disapproval, and restrictions on public credit assistance to private entities.[3]

Prior to the 1930s, most state and local bonds were supported by taxes and sold as general obligations. During the Depression, there was an increasing reliance on "special-fund" obligations, which are secured on a specific revenue source, usually a user charge. The move toward revenue bonds was stimulated by the public housing assistance programs in the 1930s and the availability of Reconstruction Finance Corporation loans. After World War II, as the definition of the public purposes eligible for tax-exempt financing was widened, there was an even more rapid growth in the use of revenue obligations, especially by special districts and authorities. From the borrowers' standpoint, the costs of improvement could be financed by users rather than by taxpayers, holding down general-obligation indebtedness.[4]

Investors have typically viewed limited-obligation bonds as being riskier than those backed by the full taxing power of governments and have demanded a higher return on such bonds.[5] But as familiarity with the revenue bond grew and as concern over creditworthiness lessened in the postwar period, the difference in interest rates between revenue bonds and general-obligation bonds waned. Between 1960 and 1975, revenue bonds as a proportion of total bond sales rose from 30 percent to nearly 50 percent (see Table 1).

Revenue bonds not only have grown more rapidly than general obligations but have also engendered new forms to finance new needs. Most notable has been the growth of the "lease-rental" revenue bond, which is secured by lease agreements between the issuing authority and the actual operator of the facility. Many lease-rental bonds, sold to finance housing, pollution control facilities, industrial development, and other projects, are carefully designed so that general units of government can finance quasi-public or private facilities outside their own debt limits. Since 1960, these issues have blossomed from practically nothing to more than $5 billion of the new issues sold in 1975.

State and local debt may also be viewed by level and type

Table 1   State and Local Borrowing by Type of Issue, Selected Years, 1960 to 1975

(BILLIONS OF DOLLARS)

	1960	1970	1972	1974	1975*
Long-term					
General-obligation	4.36	11.85	13.33	13.57	16.05
Revenue					
Utility	1.79	4.59	6.99	6.53	4.78
Special tax	0.08	0.34	0.25	0.46	4.16
Lease-rental	0.19	1.17	2.17	3.22	5.66
Total	2.07	6.10	9.40	10.21	14.61
New housing authority	0.40	0.13	0.96	0.46	—
Total long-term	6.81	18.19	23.75	24.32	30.65
Short-term	4.01	17.81	25.27	29.54	29.90

*Estimated.

Note: Because of rounding, figures may not add up to totals.

Sources: Investment Bankers Association, *Statistical Bulletin;* Securities Industry Association, *Municipal Market Developments* (various issues).

of government. As Table 2 illustrates, debt issuances by general units of government have diminished in importance with the relative growth of issues by statutory authorities and special districts. The growth in authority and special district debt and the increasing reliance on lease-rental revenue obligations are clearly intertwined.[6]

The purposes for state and local borrowing have changed emphasis as well. As shown in Table 3, loans for education, transportation, and water and sewerage, which grew rapidly through the 1960s, have declined. In 1960, bonds for these three uses amounted to 65 percent of total bond sales; by 1974, their combined share of the total had slipped to 35 percent. Borrowing for social welfare, utilities, and conservation meanwhile grew rapidly throughout the period.

Table 2   Debt Sold by Type of Issuer, 1960 to 1975

(BILLIONS OF DOLLARS)

	1960	1970	1972	1974	1975*
State	1.00	4.17	4.99	4.79	7.43
Local general government	2.54	6.21	7.25	8.66	8.29
School district	1.35	2.13	1.92	2.16	2.44
Special district	0.66	1.16	1.51	1.27	1.57
Statutory authority	1.30	4.39	8.01	7.37	10.91
Total	6.85	18.08	23.69	24.24	30.65

*Estimated.

Note: Because of rounding, figures may not add up to totals.

Source: Securities Industry Association.

Aside from the pronounced shifting of the municipal market toward more short-term borrowing (discussed more fully below), the most important development in the past 15 years has been the broadened definition of public purpose, which created numerous new instrumentalities and debt instruments.

POLLUTION BONDS: CLEANING UP . . . IN THE MARKET

The 1970s have witnessed a mushrooming in the use of the tax-exempt bond to finance a broad assortment of quasi-public and, frequently, essentially private facilities and activities. The advantages are clear: tax exemption can often provide 100 percent debt financing at interest rates often considerably lower than those of conventional securities whose interest income is taxable. Not surprisingly, government officials and private interests have found it mutually advantageous to cooperate in expanding the scope of public purpose—and the tax-exempt bond—to finance a variety of nontraditional purposes.

The most significant and controversial member of this

Table 3   Sales of State and Local Government Bonds by Use of Proceeds

(BILLIONS OF DOLLARS)

Purpose	1960	1970	1972	1974	1975
Education	2.28	5.03	4.98	4.73	4.69
Transportation	1.31	3.17	2.99	1.71	2.21
Utilities and conservation total	1.30	3.47	4.68	5.64	7.26
Water and sewerage	1.02	2.40	2.45	1.99	2.32
Pollution control (industrial)	0.00	0.00	0.60	1.71	2.23
Other utility and construction	0.28	1.07	1.64	1.94	2.71
Social welfare total	0.60	1.47	3.82	4.45	4.40
Public housing	0.43	0.13	1.92	1.69	0.65
Hospitals	na*	na*	0.50	0.78	1.96
Other	0.17	1.30	1.41	1.98	1.79
Industrial aid	0.04	0.11	0.33	0.50	0.46
Other (general purpose)	1.53	4.20	5.30	6.50	10.59
Total volume	7.11	18.56	23.69	24.24	30.65
Total new capital	7.06	18.45	22.12	23.51	29.60
Refunding	0.05	0.11	1.57	0.73	1.00

*na = not available.
Note: Because of rounding, figures may not add up to totals.

Source: Securities Industry Association.

new group of borrowings is the pollution control bond—a means of financing the pollution control expenditures of private enterprise; these bonds are an outgrowth of the industrial development bond sold by the government to build facilities for lease or resale to private companies. Such methods allow governments to finance public facilities outside their own debt limits. Industrial bonds flourished in the early and mid-1960s but were reduced to a trickle after 1969, when changes in the allowable uses of tax exemption under Section 103 of the Internal Revenue Code took effect. However, certain forms of industrial aid bonds, the most important being the pollution control bond issued on behalf of corporations to install pollution abatement facilities, survived the restriction. Congress left the door open to such bond sales if the proceeds were used to construct or acquire facilities to control air and water pollution.[7]

As the focus of national policy shifted to the problems of air and water pollution, there was an enormous resurgence in tax-exempt industrial financing in the guise of pollution control bonds. Sales of these bonds rocketed from less than $100 million in 1971 to an estimated $2.2 billion in 1975. It is further estimated that in 1974 and 1975, these bonds represented about 7 to 8 percent of all long-term municipal bond sales.[8]

The cost of the tax-exempt subsidy of pollution control is borne by the public because the federal government does not collect taxes on interest income from tax-exempt bonds and, in many cases, state and local governments also do not collect such taxes. Another cost is incurred by the other issuers of tax-exempt bonds because the increased supply of bonds pushes up interest rates. Benefits redound to the firm making the improvement and also to the buyer of tax-exempt pollution control bonds—the unintended beneficiary, who reaps a higher after-tax yield on the interest income.

Because of the large financing needs of industry in order to control pollution and the availability of the pollution control bond, most observers predict continued growth in sales through the end of the decade.[9] It has been estimated that resulting tax losses could total $640 million annually by 1980.[10] Moreover, debt service costs to sponsoring state and local governments would be an additional $150 million annually. Corporations would receive a total of $425 million in interest savings, just over half the benefit of tax exemption. The remaining tax-sheltered benefit, about $365 million annually, would go to high-income investors.

Another complaint about the pollution control bond is that it is not readily available to small borrowers; it is used primarily by large firms that could finance pollution equipment in other ways.[11] There is also concern about the pollution bond's potential for undermining the whole concept of tax exemption. Meanwhile, the heavy use of the device in a troubled municipal bond market has lessened its efficiency as a means of lowering interest costs for clean-up facilities.[12]

FINANCING OF HOSPITALS AND STADIUMS

The pollution bond may be the biggest and most controversial of the new uses found for tax exemption, but another dramatic example is the meteoric rise of tax-exempt financing of hospitals and health care facilities. In many parts of the country, ownership and operation of hospitals have long been considered public purposes, but the use of revenue bonds to finance their construction and acquisition on behalf of not-for-profit entities is a new phenomenon. In 1975, approximately $2 billion in hospital bonds were sold, up from only $500 million in 1972.

Most bonds are sold by a governmental health care authority or unit of local government on behalf of the not-for-profit hospital. The issuer acts as a lessor or mortgagee, and the hospital pledges gross revenues as security for the lease or mortgage payments. Most new issues rely upon the promise of future earning power of the new facility to encourage investors to purchase them.[13] The highly anticipatory nature of their revenue and the relative novelty of these financings have combined to lift their interest costs substantially above those of more conventional tax-exempt debt securities. But even at high rates of interest, the use of tax-exempt bonds can provide a substantial reduction—often 2 percentage points—in borrowing costs over costs in the taxable securities market.[14] Thus, the supply of such financings remains strong and is expected to grow.[15]

Perhaps the most spectacular use of tax exemption to provide for the amenities of modern life has been the financing of major office, convention, and sports complexes. In the euphoria of the 1960s, in terms of money and prestige, many cities began to see such enterprises as vital to their functions as hubs of regional and national activity. However, these facilities have proved to be risky and expensive. Typically, they depended upon revenues from leases executed with private organizations or the sponsoring government. The record pace of inflation in construction costs increased their financing beyond original expectations. With the murderous competition for teams and events, project revenues were highly unstable.

As an example of the combined impact of these factors, the New Orleans Superdome was supposed to cost $35 million when first proposed in 1966. But final costs exceeded $160 million, and the Superdome is currently operating at an annual deficit of $35 million, which is borne by Louisiana taxpayers.[16]

Nevertheless, the lure of ready capital at low interest appears to be stimulating more demand. According to a recent survey, 44 cities are planning to build or renovate sports and convention facilities to the tune of $1.5 billion, most of which will be financed with tax-exempt securities.[17]

MORTGAGING THE FUTURE

Starting with the New York Housing Finance Agency in 1960, agencies of state governments have sponsored programs to support the housing construction and mortgage markets. Originally dependent upon various federal housing subsidies, these programs kicked into high gear with the passage of the Urban Development Act in 1968 and its famous Sections 235 and 236, which allocated some money directly to state agencies. Activity swelled during the late 1960s and early 1970s until, by the end of 1975, there was $7 billion of such debt outstanding and state housing agencies existed in 46 states.

The programs take various forms, but the basic idea is the same: the government agency acts as a financial intermediary, issuing revenue bonds and using the proceeds to purchase the securities of private developers, housing companies, private financial institutions, or even individual home-owners.[18] In some cases, the agency itself may actually engage in the construction and subsequent operation or sale of the housing project.

As Table 4 illustrates, most of the state-agency housing support has taken the form of direct lending through mortgages originated by the agency, and this has been aimed almost

Table 4   Summary of Lending Activity of State Housing Finance Agencies, 1975

Program	Amount of Debt (Millions of Dollars)	Percent of Total Financing	Percent of Mortgage Lending Activity by Type of Housing	
			Single-family	Multifamily
Direct mortgage lending	$5,243.2	77.5	4.5	95.5
Purchase of mortgages	776.8	11.5 ⎫	81.4	18.6
Loans to lenders	578.3	8.5 ⎭		
Construction loans	168.5	2.5	—	100.0
Total	$6,766.8	100.0		

Source: Compiled from prospectuses and annual reports of state housing agencies.

exclusively at multifamily projects. The mortgage purchase program and loan-to-lender program (where loans are made to private lenders who, in turn, make mortgage loans), however, have focused on supporting the mortgage market for single-family dwellings.

Most state housing programs have involved federal subsidies of one form or another. However, with the ebb and flow and changing goals and design of subsidy programs, the agencies have had to stay nimble to carry out their missions. Doing this has involved developing a mind-boggling array of revenue-bond instruments. To accommodate these financings, the agencies, many of whose arrangements fall within the ambit of industrial development bonds, have been given certain exceptions under Section 103 of the Internal Revenue Code.[19]

Some programs use federal aid supplements and others are secured by various federal guarantees, but the typical state housing finance operation is a highly leveraged affair. Practically all the bond proceeds go to support the program being financed, and there is little or no "equity" capital supplied by the state. These high-risk operations spawned several ingenious devices to enhance their acceptance in the market. The most popular of these rapidly proved to be the moral obligation bond, originated by the granddaddy of the state housing agencies, the New York Housing and Finance Agency.[20]

The distinguishing feature of the moral obligation bond is its backing by a unit of government that agrees to meet any deficiency in a reserve fund established to back up the debt. The sponsoring government is morally obligated and authorized to make deficiency payments, but it is not legally liable. Hence the moral obligation is not counted as part of the debt of the unit.[21] The ability to finance projects through this back-door method proved appealing, particularly because projects supported by revenues need not be approved by public referendum.

State housing agencies were the most aggressive users of the moral obligation bond, but other applications were also found, including the repackaging of local governmental debt into consolidated issues sold by state bond banks. The moral obligation concept caught on like there was no tomorrow—and then, in 1975, tomorrow arrived.

4

1975: Confrontation in the Markets

The problems that had accumulated beneath much of the heady growth of the municipal bond market in the 1960s and 1970s began to be flushed out by the economic troubles that developed in 1974—a combination of inflation, recession, and tight credit. Ironically, the problems came home to roost in New York City and State—the large, sophisticated entities that had pioneered many of the changes in marketing methods that occurred during the 1960s. The troubles surfaced in February 1975, when the New York State Urban Development Corporation (UDC), in a double dose of irony, failed to meet short-term debt because of its inability to market its moral obligation bonds.

The ensuing turmoil in the municipal bond market was tethered to a continuing and all-consuming credit crisis in New York State. But the effects ranged far beyond the borders of that state. Investors, who had increasingly come to view all municipal bonds as secure ("money good" in the jargon of the market), watched the value of their holdings plummet, and they became obsessed with discovering and avoiding other New Yorks. For most state and local governments, the results were costly; for some, they were devastating. The moral obligation device, which had made so many projects possible, was itself undone; and short-term debt, which had enabled many governments and projects to buy now and pay later, suddenly became a cash drain rather than a cash source. Those governments with the largest debts, lowest incomes, and poorest prospects were hit the hardest.

UDC: A TEST OF MORAL OBLIGATION

The moral obligation was put to the test in March 1975, when UDC briefly defaulted on $100 million in short-term notes due. Although the state of New York ultimately stood behind the note issue, it first maintained that UDC's short-term notes were not covered by the obligation that backed the bonds, a legal distinction that did not give investors assurance of the state's intention to stand behind the corporation's financing.[1] Soon afterward, the loss of confidence in New York State's securities and the skepticism about moral obligations led to the inability of New York City and various state agencies to refinance billions of dollars in short-term loans, either by rollovers of the notes or conversion into long-term debt. The rating agencies, uncertain about the state's willingness and ability either to stand behind the notes or to refinance them, refused to give ratings to new issues and withdrew ratings on those outstanding.[2] The uncertainty in the market had a devastating effect on the housing agencies. A 1 percentage point increase in the rate that agencies must pay to borrow adds $25 per month to rents in housing projects.[3] Thus, escalating costs and the rapid rise in tax-exempt rates greatly reduced the margin between the housing agencies' cost of capital and the rates they could charge for loans or add to rents. By late 1975, the yields on long-term housing bonds had risen from their usual 60 to 70 percent to more than 80 percent of the rates on insured mortages.[4] (The problems of these agencies were further compounded by the introduction of the new Section 8 of the federal assistance program, which creates difficulties in packaging bond issues if this method of subsidy is used.)

Interruptions in financing would delay the completion not only of housing but also of other projects under way, reducing the projects' capacity to support themselves. In some cases, this would increase the need to invoke the moral obligation of the sponsoring state government. The heyday of moral obligation bonds was over—but a $9 billion legacy of problems remained.

In reaction to the plight of the housing agencies in particular, pressure was brought to bear on the federal government to find a new means of insuring the housing bonds and to help reestablish their marketability. By June 1976, the Department of Housing and Urban Development (HUD) had announced a new program that would insure up to 80 percent of the losses on mortgage defaults on multifamily projects.[5] In the same month, HUD also proposed regulations that would give state housing agencies the option to receive a federal interest subsidy payment on debt issues sold as taxable securities.[6]

WHO'S IN CHARGE?

The credit crisis in New York vividly illustrated risks inherent in a borrowing policy that had allowed public debt to accumulate beyond the capacity of a state to support that debt. The massive use of borrowing to finance worthy but expensive social goals in the private market, the triumph of optimism over realism, had proved temporary.

In New York, the special-fund doctrine and the revenue bond had been stretched to support high-risk, non-self-liquidating projects through a legion of public authorities that were not subject to the controls and restraints of traditional state departments and agencies. The supposed separation of their debt burden from that of the state proved fictitious; the supposed advantages of independence and insulation ultimately translated into a lack of accountability to and oversight by the public they had been entrusted to serve.

In early 1975, the new administration of Governor Hugh Carey of New York set about to do two things: first, to avert the financial collapse of UDC and its sister agencies and, second, to seek out the causes for its sickness and to protect against recurrence. The Moreland Act Commission on the Urban Development Corporation and Other State Financing

Agencies was created to carry out the second task. The commission filed its report in March 1976 and made many detailed recommendations, but at the heart of its analysis was the fact that nobody had really been in charge:

> The Commission's public hearings revealed that the principal institutional weaknesses in the authority device are the lack of accountability to or adequate monitoring by the Legislature, Comptroller, Executive and public, and the lack of overall State planning and debt management.[7]

In most cases, authorities have been established to carry out a public mission with a professionalism that is insulated from the rough-and-tumble of political pressures. But formal mechanisms for the periodic reassessment of the goals and purposes of these agencies have been generally absent. In some instances, the original authorizing legislation is open-ended: there are no ceilings on the potential debts that can be created.

DISARRAY IN THE SHORT-TERM MARKET

The succession of crises engulfing New York City and New York State and its agencies riveted public attention to a little-publicized but fast-growing form of credit: the municipal short-term note. In the city's case, short-term borrowing had been used to paper over a snowballing succession of operating deficits and to finance both capital and current expenditures in anticipation of bond sales. In other words, the city had used short-term borrowing to finance current deficits as an alternative to increased taxes or reductions in expenditures. New York City, which alone accounted for one-quarter (or $7 billion) of short-term note sales in 1974, was no doubt the leading, but not the only, practitioner of this use of short-term credit. The state and its agencies, particularly those involved in housing, have also used short-term loans freely to anticipate revenues and bond sales, and similar practices have flourished throughout the Northeast. It is estimated that in 1974, New York State and its jurisdictions represented 40 percent and the Northeast (including New York) represented 60 percent of all state and local short-term debt outstanding.

Borrowing short-term against *local* tax revenues expected within the revenue cycle is a widely used and accepted form of credit. In the early 1970s, a new variant of this type of borrowing developed, based on anticipation of assistance from another level of government.

The problem was particularly acute in New York State, where, because of differing budget cycles, local units in part borrowed in anticipation of state-aid payments, while the state, in turn, borrowed to make these payments prior to the receipt of its own tax revenues. By the spring of 1976, the entire paper structure of anticipation borrowing threatened to crumple, setting off defaults.

The use of bond anticipation notes also increased greatly after 1970. This poses similar problems because paying off the short-term debt depends upon the future—and now uncertain—ability of the borrower to convert the short-term liability into long-term debt. Investors became more conscious of these problems in the wake of UDC's default in February 1975. By the end of that year, the municipal note market was in serious disarray in the Eastern United States; the cost of short-term borrowing leaped by 2 to 5 percentage points for borrowers in New York State because of credit concerns.[8]

THE SPECIAL PLIGHT OF OLDER CITIES

The New York crisis had an immediate impact on the older cities in the industrial crescent that extends through the Northeast to the Great Lakes. The bond ratings of a number of these cities had been reduced in the 1960s, but Philadelphia, Buffalo, Boston, Cleveland, Baltimore, Detroit, and other cities, along with New York, retained reasonably good access to the credit markets. Some maintained or even improved their credit standing in the face of strong indications that their local economies were deteriorating.[9] The unnerving events of 1975, however, forced the market to take another look at the basic economic prospects of the major cities.

The cities' prospects have worsened over the past decade. With the losses in population in several major Eastern and Midwestern cities, the remaining populations have become increasingly composed of older and relatively less affluent people.[10] Twenty-three of the 24 largest cities have shown a relative increase in the proportion of the nation's poor living within their boundaries. Private employment—which ultimately must sustain the local tax base—has declined as industry and jobs have fled to suburbia, exurbia, or the Sun Belt.[11] By June 1974, 21 of the 24 largest cities had unemployment rates higher than the national average.[12]

Problems of declining economic bases and growing high-need populations have been compounded by the rapidly rising costs of governmental services. Wages for employees in state and local government have risen more rapidly than in the private sector. A special problem created by these rising costs has been the strain placed on public employee pensions. Through either inertia or an effort to hold down taxes, many local governments have failed to set aside funds for the pension liabilities accrued by employees. These huge unfunded liabilities have now become a matter of increasing concern to bondholders and politicians alike. As an example, preliminary estimates indicate that unfunded pension liabilities amount to $10 billion in the state of Massachusetts, including $1 billion for the city of Boston.[13]

City governments have been particularly hard hit by the recent high rates of inflation. Although local governments appear to come out slightly ahead in periods of mild inflation, the hyperinflation of 1973 and 1974 caused estimated tax bases to grow by only 15 percent, while expenditures (held constant at 1972 levels of real goods and services) shot up by 25 percent. As a result, between 1972 and 1974, state and local purchasing power declined by about 10 percent.[14] Thus, local tax bases were incapable of stabilizing real spending levels, much less of supporting higher levels of real public goods and services. Because fuel costs were already higher in the Northeast, an area already in economic difficulties, the cost effects of the energy crisis were particularly adverse.[15]

Outside help was limited. Federal aid surged with revenue sharing in 1972, but many cities found that revenue sharing was often only a substitute for categorical assistance that was impounded or terminated. Moreover, the states did not show much interest in assuming the more costly functions of the cities.[16]

In late 1973 and 1974, rising costs and sluggish revenues generally resulted in growing deficits for state and local governments, which, by the last quarter of 1974, were accumulating a deficit at a rate of $16 billion a year. (This trend continued throughout 1975. For the first three quarters of that year, the deficit was $13 billion.[17])

As inflation was aggravated by recession, the states and cities with the weakest financial conditions obviously had to take the most extreme austerity measures to balance outlays with declining income. Not surprisingly, local governments in the energy-exporting and agricultural regions of the country (the Western and South Central regions) were mostly spared; they enjoyed substantial surpluses and strong revenues.[18] But governments in high unemployment areas, with little or no surplus in their operating budgets, sank into deficits because taxes could not be raised nor expenditures cut back quickly enough.

Those cities in the worst shape were also those with the greatest debt and the highest interest costs. In fiscal 1974, large cities that were losing population had an average of 60 percent more debt than those increasing in population—and New York City had nearly *five times* more. Contributing to this phenomenon were higher building costs, more services, and a penchant for borrowing to avoid tax increases that were either impolitic or economically counterproductive. Those with the least had borrowed the most.[19]

ROUGH ROAD AHEAD

At the midpoint of the 1970s, it was becoming clearer that it was not just isolated older and poorly run cities that were in trouble. As the evidence of the recent economic changes and trends began to be studied, the systemic nature of the ills emerged. In particular, the entire Northeast quadrant of the country, ranging from New England's mill towns to the ponderous manufacturing complexes of the Midwest, showed symptoms of being a potential economic disaster area.

The causes of decline are complex and pervasive and in many respects represent the workings of an orthodox, if painful, adjustment to changing markets, processes, and values in the economy.

Much of the Northeast, which had relied heavily on manufacturing and a vast pool of associated labor skills, had never rebounded from the recession of the 1970s. As the rate of investment in the region dropped off, the plants and equipment became older and less efficient. The relatively high-cost labor force was rapidly becoming older and less mobile. Whatever new investment did occur tended to take place in high-technology industry that offered fewer jobs.[20]

The erosion in economic base and employment had been somewhat masked by the growth of governmental employment in some areas, but the phenomenon of a growing public sector to offset a declining private one proved unsustainable. As industry moved to the less expensive sites and work forces and to the developing markets of the Sun Belt, the Northeast lost its ability to export the costs of government to the rest of the country. The situation was compounded by the dramatic surge in the cost of energy, of which the price per unit soared to 3½ times the national average in New England.[21]

The opportunities for self-help appeared limited in the face of such fundamental changes in the terms of competitive advantage. Governments that reduced expenditures might lower taxes—but only at the cost of swelling unemployment rates and decaying facilities. But the converse approach—spending more and taxing more—threatened to drive away the tax-paying elements needed to promote sustainable growth, leaving the high-cost populations in disproportionate supply.[22]

Furthermore, the fractionalized political structure of much of the region hampered the declining central city in its pursuit of revenues beyond its legal boundaries. Such boundaries actually provide incentives for businesses to move into relatively well-heeled suburbs, which escape the costs and problems of the decaying urban core.[23]

By the outset of 1976, the growing disparities not only among cities, but also among entire regions of the country, were threatening to incite a new "war between the states," with the have-not areas actively struggling to recapture productive industry and populations.[24] Federal policy to cope with this phenomenon was inadequate, if not perverse. As economic activity shifted to the South and West, the long-standing favorable differentials in federal payments versus taxes to these areas came under severe questioning.[25] Looking into their own limited arsenals of economic development, those states on the losing end began to organize themselves and take a new interest in such things as tax incentives and development bonds and in generally promoting a favorable, cost-cutting environment for business. Doubt remained as to whether or not such a competition could be waged without disrupting the fabric of a highly interdependent economy and undermining the already weakened revenue structure of many governments; but to the state and local contestants, there seemed no other alternatives, and time was running out.[26]

5

Financing State and Local Capital Formation

Although the older and more urban regions have been the hardest hit by the recent shocks to the financial markets, state and local governmental borrowing and capital outlays have long been sensitive to changing national economic and monetary conditions. Most long-term governmental borrowing finances capital improvements such as roads, sewers, and buildings. Although the links between the actual borrowing of money and its expenditure on capital goods may be complicated and lengthy, sooner or later a high cost of borrowing or a stoppage of credit will result in trimmed or canceled projects—or in higher taxes and charges to cover an increased debt service, if a government believes it can afford them.

The rate of growth in state and local government capital spending has been tapering off since the late 1960s. The rate of increase in fixed capital expenditures, which had been running at about 10 percent a year in the mid-1960s, dropped to only 4 percent between 1968 and 1972. Moreover, the rapid escalation in the cost of construction and equipment steadily ate away at the physical substance of such outlays: between 1968 and 1973, the price-deflated or real amount of public capital formation actually declined at a rate of 2.5 percent a year.[1] Although there was, subsequently, a temporary surge of construction spending caused by the influx of federal aid, by early 1976, it appeared that a combination of factors— led by the high cost of credit and sagging fiscal prospects—

would continue to put a damper on many state and local projects.

Tight credit and rising interest rates, common in the past decade, have adversely affected governmental capital formation.[2] Major studies of the links between financial markets have identified a significant correlation between rising interest rates and decreasing bond sales. For example, these studies indicate that, after isolating other factors, a 10 percent change in borrowing costs induces a 4 to 6 percent decrease in new issues of municipal bonds.[3] The ultimate effect of rising interest rates on capital outlays has been somewhat less significant because many units have temporizing alternatives that, for moderate periods of time, can insulate spending plans from changes in the credit markets.

The relationship between interest rates and spending plans appears to vary with the size of the borrower and the available financing alternatives. Small units and those with limited alternative sources of funds show the greatest tendency to cut spending plans when faced with high rates of interest. Although most governments have been able to keep their spending plans on track, this has often been achieved by a combination of short-term borrowing and drawing on financial assets. However, as the New York situation amply demonstrated, when the short-term markets close and liquid assets are depleted, projects must be stopped.

There have been other important factors in the slowdown in capital formation by governments. One major factor has been the shift in priorities to current operating outlays for social welfare programs. The growth in federal funds for capital projects has been slower and more erratic than that for social welfare programs.[4] The growth in federal funds for capital projects has been slower and more erratic than that for other forms of federal assistance, partly because of impoundments by the federal government. To some extent, capital spending was rejuvenated by the inflow of federal revenue sharing funds and by increases in categorical assistance in 1973 and 1974. But as budgets tightened, it became clear that this effect was short-lived and that any spare funds would soon find their way into ongoing operations.

Early estimates indicate that tightening bond markets, the leveling of federal grants, and widespread stringency in the financial condition of state and local governments will continue to restrain capital expenditures from growing to any noticeable extent in the near future.[5]

CAPITAL SPENDING IN THE SECOND HALF OF THE 1970s

What will be the level of capital spending and borrowing by state and local governments during the remainder of the 1970s? To forecast this, many assumptions must be made about the real forces of demand for capital goods by state and local governments: how these demands will be constrained by the overall financial resources of governments and, as a result, how much the capital markets will be called upon to finance capital spending through the sale of state and local debt. The needs of other sectors also must be considered: Will the capital markets, as they work to match the supply and demand for funds, have the capacity to meet the desires of all? Intense competition for funds could again generate rates of interest governments cannot afford or are reluctant to pay, crowding these borrowers out of the market.

Several recent projections of state and local spending and borrowing for capital needs through 1980 are shown in Table 5. These studies assume that, as in the past, the bulk of future nonfederal public financing will be for the construction of public facilities, and they foresee a rise in the level of state and local spending and borrowing over the next few years, anticipating that reductions in real capital outlays for schools and highways, coupled with only moderate growth in other traditional spending categories, will be offset to some degree by increased spending on pollution control and mass transit.

Bosworth, Duesenberry, and Carron In their study for the Brookings Institution, *Capital Needs in the Seventies*, Barry Bosworth, James S. Duesenberry, and Andrew S. Carron foresee capital spending staging a comeback through the remainder of the decade. Construction outlays for waste treatment and mass transit, they believe, will more than offset slowdowns in

Table 5   Projection of Selected State and Local Government Outlays and Borrowing: 1980

(BILLIONS OF DOLLARS)

Source	GNP	Total Expenditures	Capital Outlays	Long-term Borrowing	Total Debt
Tax Foundation*	2,140	326	58.4	35.0	285
Bosworth et al.†	2,387	381	66.6	33.0	292
Fortune‡	2,533	na	69.1	36.5	na
Taylor§	2,418	373	na	41.7	351
Ott and Ott¶	2,428	399	55.0	31.0	na

*Tax Foundation, *The Financial Outlook for State and Local Governments to 1980* (1972). GNP: 8% annual growth rate, 1970 to 1980 (p. 25). Expenditures: $320 billion adjusted by ratio of expenditures as defined by the Bureau of the Census to those defined by the Department of Commerce in National Income Accounts, 1.018 for fiscal and calendar year 1973, respectively (p. 75). Capital outlays, borrowing debt: original figures adjusted to calendar year by 1973 ration of 1.008 (pp. 100–101).

†B. Bosworth, J. Duesenberry, and A. Carron, *Capital Needs in the Seventies* (1975). GNP: 9.2% annual growth rate, 1973 to 1980 (p. 12). Other items are as published (pp. 35, 57).

‡P. Fortune, "The Financial Impact of the Federal Water Pollution Control Act: The Case for Municipal Bond Reform" (1975). GNP: 9.0% annual growth. Capital outlays derived from adjustment of construction expenditures by 1.180 (Table 3); borrowing calculated from values on Table 3 and equations (Table 2); $4.5 billion in borrowing is for pollution control purposes (Table 7).

§S. Taylor, "A Financial Background for Project Independence" (1974). Current dollar GNP: 9.2% annual growth rate, 1974 to 1980 (Table 1); expenditure (Table 1), borrowing $25.8 billion, net flow (Table 3) plus $15.9 billion long-term debt requirements; debt (Table 5).

¶D. Ott and A. Ott, *State-Local Finances in the Last Half of the 1970's* (1975). Current dollar GNP: 9.0% annual growth rate, 1974 to 1980 (p. 91). Expenditures (Table 5-2); adjustment to a capital outlay base. Borrowing calculated from Equation E. 12, p. 28.

school and highway construction, thus increasing total capital spending by nearly 10 percent per year between 1973 and 1980. This would be significantly higher than the 7 percent growth rate of the 1960s[6] and would reverse the decline in real capital spending of the last six years.

An important assumption in the Brookings projections is that a large part of this increased capital spending will be financed by federal grants, which, the authors estimate, will support 26 percent of state and local capital outlays by 1980.

Furthermore, an increasing use of other nonborrowed funds (mainly revenues) is anticipated. As a result, bond sales for capital purposes are expected to grow at only 7 percent per annum through the late 1970s, as opposed to the 7.5 percent rate of increase in the 1960s and 11 percent in the 1950s.[7]

Two points that can be challenged in the Brookings study are the heavy reliance on nondebt sources of capital financing and the projected deficit in the state and local sectors. If the composition of financial sources were to remain the same in 1980 as it was in 1973, bond sales would equal $42 billion instead of the $33 billion projected. And if the state and local sectors experience an $18 billion deficit by 1980, as the Brookings study suggests, it is likely that pressure on current revenues for current outlays will be too great to permit much financing of capital expenditures from revenues.

Tax Foundation Projections by the Tax Foundation contrast sharply to those of the Brookings study. The foundation anticipates not only that there will be a lower level of total state and local capital expenditures but that borrowing will be a much more significant source of funds for outlays than in the past—60 percent, compared with 50 percent. In general, this study illustrates the levels of capital outlays and demands for borrowing that could be expected if the general economy and state and local sectors were to grow more slowly and reflects the spending and revenue patterns of the 1960s.[8]

The Tax Foundation study shares with the Brookings study the assumption that there will be high levels of federal grants. The Brookings study puts such grants at $67 billion annually by 1980, the Tax Foundation at $63 billion. It must be pointed out that this assumption is increasingly less realistic. The $17.1 billion in federal capital grants forecast by the Brookings study would require a 12.5 percent rate of growth over the next five years in order to rise from the level of $9.5 billion budgeted for federal grants in fiscal 1975.[9]

Ott and Ott A relatively optimistic view of the financial condition of the state and local sectors is presented by David and Attiat Ott. Their study foresees fewer difficulties in meeting capital financing needs. The Otts assume a relatively moderate rate of real growth and inflation and relatively low levels of capital outlay requirements because of demographic changes; as a result, the sectors will move toward budget surpluses. Like the Brookings and Tax Foundation analysts, they conclude that federal grants will play a major role in meeting most environmental and mass transit financing needs and in reducing the need for borrowing.[10]

Fortune and Taylor   The largest estimates of state and local borrowing needs in 1980 are contained in two other recent projections, one by Peter Fortune and the other by Steven Taylor. Notably, Fortune allows for approximately $15 billion in tax-exempt industrial pollution control bond sales over the last half of the 1970s.[11] Taylor predicts a high 12 percent annual rate of increase in state and local net borrowing— greater than that experienced in the 1960s.[12] This prediction assumes growing federal surpluses in a high investment economy geared to meet capital spending and borrowing needs.

Like the Brookings study, the Taylor study integrates state and local borrowing needs into the total demand for capital in the economy. Using somewhat different base years, each study projects a gross national product of approximately $2.4 trillion by 1980 and a generally higher level of private and domestic investment than that of the late 1960s and early 1970s. The two studies share a common assumption that the federal government will run surpluses.

RECEPTIVITY OF THE MARKETS

What will happen to the potential claims of different sectors in the capital markets? How will the competition for credit be affected? The Brookings authors make a major assumption that higher levels of business borrowing will be largely offset by a slower growth in state and local government debt and by a decline in the volume of publicly held federal debt. Generally, the Brookings study is sanguine about the ability of the capital markets to absorb the moderate increase in state and local debt through the traditional source of demand—commerical banks and individuals with high incomes.[13] Projecting a much higher level of net municipal borrowing, the Taylor study sees commercial bank holdings being supplanted by the increased holdings of individuals and by direct federal loans.[14]

But will these patterns hold up? As noted earlier in this chapter, cyclical changes in monetary conditions have a profound impact upon demand for tax-exempts. As the market is presently constituted, future monetary cycles will likely be characterized by wide swings in the cost and availability of credit to state and local governments. The concentration of municipal bond ownership in the hands of commercial banks, insurance companies, and households, as shown in Table 6, makes the market extremely vulnerable to sudden shifts in demand by any one of the three sectors.

VOLATILITY OF BANK INVESTMENT

Bank ownership of state and local government securities grew from 25 percent of outstanding issues in 1960 to 48.6 percent in 1970. At the end of 1975, commercial banks held $103 billion of these securities. The increase in the proportion of municipals held by banks between 1960 and 1970 reflects fundamental changes in bank demand that enabled these institutions to digest two-thirds of the net increase in tax-exempt securities over the decade.

The long-term trends tend to wash short-term fluctuations. The volatility of bank behavior in the market throughout the period is seen in Table 7, which shows short-run changes in net purchases of municipal securities by the three major investors. In periods of high and rising interest rates and tight credit (as in 1966, 1969, and 1974–75), demand by commercial banks for municipals drops sharply. Net purchases under such conditions have declined to as little as 2 percent of the total

Table 6   Ownership of Outstanding State and Local Government Securities, Year-End, Selected Years, 1950 to 1975

	1950	1955	1960	1965	1970	1975
				(BILLIONS OF DOLLARS)		
Commercial banks	8.4	13.1	17.7	38.9	70.2	103.1
Households	9.0	19.2	30.8	36.4	45.6	81.6
Non-life insurance companies	1.1	4.2	8.1	11.3	17.8	35.0
Other financial intermediaries	1.6	2.9	4.7	4.3	4.4	6.7
Nonfinancial corporate businesses	0.7	1.2	2.4	4.6	2.2	4.5
State and local governments	3.6	5.2	7.2	4.8	4.3	4.5
Total outstanding	24.4	45.9	70.8	100.3	144.5	235.4
				(PERCENT)		
Commercial banks	34.5	28.6	25.0	38.8	48.6	43.8
Households	36.9	41.8	43.5	36.3	31.6	34.7
Non-life insurance companies	4.7	9.1	11.4	11.3	12.3	14.9
Other financial intermediaries	6.6	6.4	6.6	4.3	3.1	2.8
Nonfinancial corporate businesses	2.7	2.7	3.4	4.6	1.5	1.9
State and local governments	14.7	11.3	10.1	4.8	3.0	1.9

Note: Because of rounding, figures may not add up to totals.

Source: Board of Governors of the Federal Reserve System, *Flow of Funds Accounts.*

Table 7   Annual Changes in Holdings of Municipal Bonds, 1960 to 1975

(BILLIONS OF DOLLARS)

Year	Commercial Banks	Fire and Casualty Insurance Companies	House-holds	Other	Total Change
1960	0.7	0.8	3.5	3.0	5.3
1961	2.8	1.0	1.2	1.0	5.1
1962	5.7	0.8	−1.0	−0.1	5.4
1963	3.9	0.7	1.0	0.1	5.7
1964	3.6	0.4	2.6	−0.6	6.0
1965	5.2	0.4	1.7	0.0	7.3
1966	2.3	1.3	3.6	−1.6	5.6
1967	9.1	1.4	−2.2	−1.5	7.8
1968	8.6	1.0	−0.8	0.7	9.5
1969	0.2	1.2	9.6	−1.1	9.9
1970	10.7	1.5	−0.8	−0.1	11.3
1971	12.6	3.9	−0.2	1.3	17.6
1972	7.2	4.8	1.0	1.4	14.4
1973	5.7	3.9	4.3	−0.2	13.7
1974	5.5	1.8	10.0	0.1	17.4
1975	1.3	2.1	10.1	1.9	15.4

Source: Board of Governors of the Federal Reserve System, *Flow of Funds Accounts.*

change in debt outstanding. By contrast, in periods when interest rates are low or declining and credit conditions are easing, bank demand for municipals picks up. In 1967, bank net purchases actually exceeded the net new issues of securities by state and local governments.

BEHAVIOR OF THE HOUSEHOLD AND BUSINESS SECTORS

Historically, the household sector's holdings of municipal securities have shown a change opposite to that of bank holdings. Throughout the 1950s, the household sector was the dominant source of funds for state and local borrowers. This role changed abruptly during the 1960s. Tax-exempts held by the household sector grew only half as fast as total outstanding issues and at one-fourth the rate of growth in bank holdings. Since 1961, the household sector appears to have acted as a residual source of funds for state and local debt. After the demands of commercial banks and casualty companies have been satisfied, municipal borrowers and their underwriters have turned increasingly to individuals to purchase their securities. In some years, notably 1969 and 1975, the remaining supply has been substantial, and individuals have been called upon to purchase as much as 96 percent of the new issues.

After having fallen to a low of 25 percent in 1972, the proportion of municipals held by the household sector has begun to grow and now equals approximately 35 percent of outstanding issues—but the cost of attracting investment by the household sector has been high. As Chart 1 shows, the years in which individuals have provided the greatest support for the tax-exempt market are also the years in which the rates of interest on these securities, compared with taxable securities, have been generally high. Thus, individuals are attracted to the tax-exempt market under conditions least favorable for state and local borrowers. Conversely, when institutional investors have ample funds and their appetite for municipals is healthy, the ratio of tax-exempt to taxable bond interest rates goes down.

Property and casualty companies, the other major institutional investors in municipals, do not appear to have a systematic pattern of cyclical investment. Nevertheless, there are rather pronounced shifts in the annual flow of funds from these companies, ranging from a low of $400 million, or 5 percent of the total change in municipal debt outstanding in 1965, to nearly $5 billion, or 28 percent, in 1972. Fluctuations of this magnitude are serious because insurance company behavior can either complement or substitute for bank demand, thereby intensifying or easing pressures on municipal bond interest rates. Property and casualty insurance companies have become an increasingly important source of investment funds for tax-exempt borrowers. Their share of the market has more than tripled since 1950. Table 6 indicates that portfolio holdings for the insurance company sector

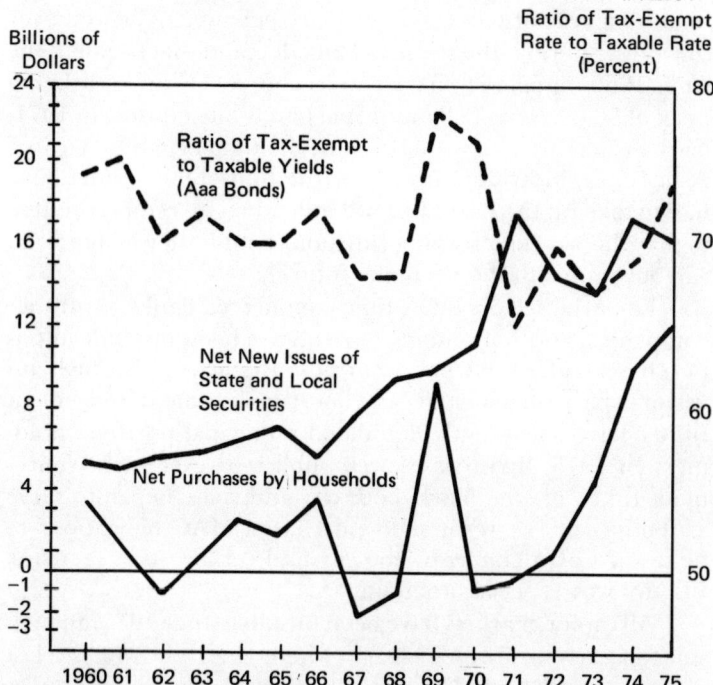

Sources: Board of Governors of the Federal Reserve System, *Flow of Funds Accounts*; ratio of tax-exempt to taxable yields derived from interest rate series in *Moody's Bond Record.*

Chart 1   Net New Issues of Municipals, Household Purchases, and the Tax-Exempt/Taxable Interest Rate Ratio

(other than life insurance companies) have generally outpaced the rate of growth in total outstanding municipal debt.

WHO WILL TAKE UP THE SLACK?

A matter of great concern is whether or not the historical investment cycle has weakened, for this raises serious questions about future demand in the market. Bank demand remained quiescent in 1975, even though business demand for loans in a year of recession was extremely weak. Viewed over the longer period, the surge in bank demand that began in the early 1960s appears to have run its course. Having reached a peak of 50 percent of all municipal bonds outstanding in 1971, bank ownership as a proportion of the total began to decline. As a result, individual investors (the household sector) have had to take up the slack. But will individual investors continue to play this shock-absorbing function? And if they do not, who will buy municipal bonds in the future?

Financial sectors other than commercial banks, insurance companies, and households have always been insignificant as purchasers of municipal securities. In fact, many such investors, particularly state and local government retirement funds, have consistently liquidated municipal portfolio holdings. In 1975, there was a well-publicized exception: retirement funds in New York, both city and state, began to serve as lenders of last resort and purchased MAC obligations to help ward off defaults by the city and certain state agencies. But this was a special situation.

All capital markets have been unstable since 1971, and it is still too early to foresee clearly where the trends of the last few years will lead. However, total bank demand for tax-exempt securities appears to be stagnating. No institutional buyer of tax-exempts has stepped forward to fill the gap. Instead, the demand for municipals has been met by the market in the traditional way—by offering higher interest rates to attract new or marginal investors.

6

Investor Demand for Municipals: Who Buys the Bonds?

The volatility of the market demand for municipal bonds is intensified by the tax-exemption feature of these securities, which is at once their chief attraction to investors and the cause for periodic episodes of weak market performance. As observed earlier in this paper, municipal bonds are not the preferred investment of any of the three chief buyers. Robert Huefner has noted that the volatile behavior of bank investment is a consequence of the inferior and residual role that tax-exempt securities often occupy within the pecking order of assets available to banks:

> Banks have strong priorities in their investments, these priorities being first the legally required reserves and second the loan demands of their customers. Their investment in municipal securities comes from their residual funds, if any. And the investment so made is then subject to future liquidation if the priority investments demand more funds than otherwise available.[1]

Different conditions and objectives trigger the heavy purchase of municipal bonds by the other two major buyers—the fire and casualty insurance companies and the household sector. But in each case, market behavior is fundamentally conditioned by a greater or lesser need for tax-sheltered income. This chapter is devoted to an examination of the determinants of buyer behavior and the way in which the patterns of behavior are changing.

COMMERCIAL BANK DEMAND FOR TAX-EXEMPT SECURITIES

Commercial banks are the major financial intermediaries, subject to federal income taxes at full corporate tax rates. They have a special incentive to increase the flow of operating earnings to after-tax income because after-tax income is the basis for growth in equity capital, which determines bank lending capacity.[2]

Banks are generally precluded from the popular methods of tax avoidance available to other investors. For example, banks must pay ordinary income tax on capital gains from transactions in fixed-income securities, and common stocks are not generally permitted as a form of investment.[3] Thus, by what amounts to a process of elimination, tax-exempt municipal securities have become the principal financial asset available to commercial banks for sheltering income from taxes.

The explosive growth in bank demand for municipal securities during the 1960s resulted from a greater awareness of the value of tax-exempt income and can be viewed as catch-up demand.[4] However, some fundamental changes in asset and liability management also led to more extensive investments in tax-exempt securities.

Perhaps the signal event in this period was the widespread introduction of the negotiable certificate of deposit in 1961.[5] The ready appeal of this short-term, interest-bearing instrument to corporations and others with temporarily idle cash balances sparked a tremendous increase in time and savings deposits at commercial banks, with corresponding increases in interest expenses. To cover added costs, banks became more venturesome, seeking out higher-yielding assets. This drive was reinforced by the notion of liability management, which held that the liquidity needed to meet withdrawals or to expand loans could be "purchased" as long as banks were willing to buy funds in the open market. As a logical concomitant of this philosophy of funds management, there was less concern about maintaining a substantial secondary reserve of such highly liquid assets as U.S. Treasury bills because they would provide only redundant liquidity.

These developments are illustrated by the changes that took place in bank balance sheet ratios, shown in Table 8. Between 1960 and 1974, time deposits compared with total assets increased from 28.5 to 46.3 percent. The drive for higher earnings is reflected in the declining ratio of investments to total assets and in the increased proportion of assets allocated for other loans with higher interest rates.

Within the investment portfolio, an even more pronounced shift has occurred. The pressure for growth in income, together with a revised view of the role of secondary asset reserves for liquidity purposes, has fostered a massive shift from U.S. Treasury securities to municipal securities with their higher after-tax yields. Municipal securities in December 1974 accounted for more than 50 percent of all bank investments, more than double the portfolio share in 1960. Even though securities investments as a whole have shrunk in comparison with total assets, the proportion of municipals has almost doubled from 6.8 percent of assets in 1960 to 12 percent in 1970, receding slightly to 11 percent at the end of 1974.

The close association between holdings of municipal

Table 8 Selected Balance Sheet Ratios for All Insured Commercial Banks

(PERCENT)

	1960	1965	1970	1974
Time deposits/total assets	28.5	39.3	40.8	46.3
Investments/total assets	31.6	27.6	25.5	21.3
State and local securities/total assets	6.8	10.3	12.0	11.0
State and local securities/total investments	21.4	37.1	47.1	51.7
State and local securities/time deposits	23.9	26.2	29.4	23.8

Note: Year-end data.

Source: Federal Deposit Insurance Corporation, *Annual Reports* (various issues).

securities and time deposits can be seen in the reasonably stable ratio between the two between 1960 and 1974. This reflects in part the unique ability of banks to finance investments in municipals by deducting the interest expense on funds borrowed to acquire tax-exempt securities.[6]

It is doubtful that there will be another spurt in bank purchases of municipals similar to that of the 1960s. Alternative money-market instruments such as mutual funds now compete with banks' negotiable time deposits for short-term, "safe" investable funds. Moreover, bankers realize that there are limits to liquidity that can be purchased through management of liabilities. The liquidity crunch of 1974 reemphasized the painful fact that the size of the banking system ultimately is determined by federal monetary authorities.

Also militating against a resurgence of growth in bank purchases of municipal securities is the peculiar vulnerability of tax-exempt bond prices to unexpected jumps in interest rates. The precipitous declines in the value of bank-owned tax-exempt securities have underlined another painful side effect of the drive to maximize commercial bank earnings: higher returns have been achieved in part by adding riskier assets to portfolios.

The pattern of municipal purchases within the banking sector also suggests that the heyday of bank demand will not soon be repeated. The growth in bank holdings in the early 1960s was particularly evident at large banks. Holdings of the 100 largest banks increased at an annual rate of 21 percent from 1960 to 1965; these institutions held 47 percent of all bank-owned municipals by December 1965. Between 1965 and 1974, however, they added to their tax-exempt holdings at the much lower annual rate of 6.25 percent, and by 1974, they accounted for but 33 percent of all bank holdings.[7]

Ironically, the early surge in tax-exempt investments is partly responsible for satiating the appetite of large institutions. However, large banks have also been the most aggressive in pursuing other forms of tax shelters, such as leasing and foreign bank operations. Leasing, for example, is mainly an enterprise of larger bank-holding companies. Under direct lease financing, commercial banks acquire equity positions as owners and lessors of physical assets such as oil tankers, jet aircraft, and railroad rolling stock. Banks generally finance the purchase of these "real" assets by selling loan participations to other institutional investors, reducing the actual bank equity position to as little as 15 or 20 percent of the purchase price. For this proportionately small equity position, the bank owner-lessor receives all the tax benefits. Specifically, banks can apply accelerated depreciation methods and investment tax credits based on the full purchase price of the asset to reduce the proportion of operating income subject to taxation.[8]

Foreign tax credits against domestic taxation have been the paradoxical outcome of an earlier attempt to improve the United States balance of payments. As Donald Mullineaux explains, "the match in the powder barrel setting off the explosion in foreign-based bank operations"[9] was the advent of the Voluntary Foreign Credit Restraint Program (VFCR) in 1965. The program was designed to help the United States balance of payments by placing limits on the amounts of loan-able funds that United States banks could transfer abroad. As a result, banks channeled funds directly to their foreign branches in order to loan them without violating VFCR guidelines. The number of United States banks operating overseas offices jumped from 11 in 1964 to 108 in 1972, and by 1973, foreign branch deposits accounted for nearly 30 percent of total deposits of those banks operating abroad, compared with only 6 percent in 1964. The effect on profits has been even more significant. Foreign income has grown at a compound annual rate of 45 percent for the largest 10 banks and accounts for half of the total profits for some of these banks.[10] Taxes paid to foreign governments on income from overseas operations, although incorporated in the "worldwide" tax burden on commercial banks, can be used to offset the domestic tax burden. Consequently, multinational banking activities compete with municipal securities as sources of after-tax income.[11]

These wide-ranging multinational activities have eroded an important segment of overall bank demand for municipal securities. Between 1970 and 1974, for example, the proportion of municipal securities to total assets held by the 100 largest banks was sliced in half, from 11.4 to 5.7 percent, and actual holdings of tax-exempts declined by $1.4 billion between December 1972 and December 1974.[12]

Another change in the composition of bank demand for municipal securities is in desired maturities of issues to be purchased. Traditionally, large institutions have bought significant amounts of long-term maturities, whereas smaller banks have been more interested in balancing the maturity structure of their portfolios with short- and intermediate-term debt. As noted in a detailed study of the maturity profile of bank investments in 1972:

> Large banks in states with important financial centers hold the bulk of the longest-term obligations and, at the opposite end of the maturity range, a large share of the tax warrants as well. New York and California, with 15% and 8%, respectively, of total U.S. municipal obligations, hold 49% and 21%, respectively, of all those maturing after 30 years; no other state holds more than 4%. For all insured commercial banks in the United States, 80% of these long-term obligations are held by 53 of the 83 banks whose total assets are more than $1 billion.[13]

The decreasing desire of the large commercial banks for tax-exempt securities implies further erosion in the congenitally weak demand for longer-term bonds.[14]

The countercyclical pattern of total bank demand for municipals—additions to municipal bond portfolios have tended to be most sizable during periods of slack business-loan demand—was reversed during the recent economic recession. In 1975, commercial banks were reluctant to make major commitments in the tax-exempt market and instead redirected massive inflows of funds from loan repayments into the short-term United States government market.[15] Such portfolio management indicates growing concern among bank managers and regulators about the liquidity and quality of bank assets, and it also reflects a more pessimistic view of whether or not liabilities can be managed aggressively and safely, given the vicissitudes of the money market.

PURCHASES BY FIRE AND CASUALTY COMPANIES

Fire and casualty companies' appetite for tax-exempts depends both on the availability of investable funds and on the need for tax shelters. Generally, these companies buy tax-exempts only when they need to shelter profits that otherwise would be taxable at the full marginal corporate rate. The level of municipal bond purchases can be linked directly to the level of policyholders' surplus.[16] When industry profits decline, these intermediaries generally seek to improve cash flow by shifting to taxable investments bearing higher interest rates.

Fire and casualty companies buy for yield rather than liquidity. As seen in Table 9, they typically place more than 50 percent of their municipal portfolio holdings into revenue bonds, which have higher yields and longer maturities than general obligation issues. Because of their buying patterns, these companies are especially important to the market for

Table 9   Type of Tax-Exempt Securities Held by Property and Casualty Insurance Companies

(PERCENT)

	1968	1970	1972
State	15.5	17.3	20.8
Political subdivision	28.4	27.7	26.4
Special revenue	56.1	55.1	52.8
Total	100.0	100.0	100.0

Note: Because of rounding, figures may not add up to totals.

Source: Data files of New York State Department of Insurance.

longer-term bonds and lower-rated revenue bond issues. Casualty insurance companies have had a particularly keen appetite for tax-exempt pollution control bonds. One survey found that 18 large insurance companies with 57 percent of industry assets purchased 55 percent of the volume of pollution control bonds sold in 1973. Practically all of these bonds had terms of 20 to 30 years, and these purchases accounted for 30 percent of all tax-exempt acquisitions by these companies in 1973.[17]

Property and casualty companies were unusually active in the municipal bond market between 1971 and 1973, acquiring nearly 30 percent of net new issues. But in 1974, the 3,000 companies in the industry experienced record underwriting losses, including policyholder dividends of about $2.7 billion. In 1975, losses soared by 70 percent to an estimated $4.5 billion, and 30 companies went out of business.[18] Participation in the municipal bond market dropped sharply.

The recent poor performance of the industry is attributed to a combination of inflation and regulatory lag. Increased outlays were required to satisfy claims, but the companies were unable to raise premiums to cover these higher costs. No-fault insurance has also had a depressing effect; because of the rapid adjudication and prompt settlement of claims, the floating amount of investable funds has been reduced. Although the industry may be bringing losses under control and entering a period of recovery, there is no reason to anticipate a more sustained or stable growth in earnings or, therefore, to expect a sustained high level of demand for municipal bonds.[19]

HOUSEHOLDS' LACK OF SUSTAINED INTEREST

The household sector provides an important but residual source of funds for the municipal market, which comes into play only when interest rates in general are high and when commercial banks are withdrawing from the market. Evidently, the lure of tax-exempt income is insufficient to draw more than a nominal amount of regular, sustained buying interest.

As Table 10 shows, municipal securities represent only 3 percent of all financial assets held by the household sector over the past 25 years. It has been estimated that the average marginal tax rate for individual investors in tax-exempts is approximately 55 percent and that about 70 percent of the municipal bonds held by households are owned by investors with incomes of $50,000 or more.[20] Between 1962 and 1972, the gross incomes of individuals taxed at a marginal rate of at least 50 percent have been growing by 9 percent annually. Yet holdings of the entire household sector in tax-exempt debt had a much lower growth rate—only 4 percent annually.[21] At first glance, this slow rate of growth is surprising. Under our progressive system of taxation, the effects of inflation and real income gains should push more and more investors into higher marginal tax brackets and boost demand for tax-exempt income. What are the reasons for the uninspired market participation by individuals?

As is seen in Table 10, time deposits have accounted for a growing share of household assets. This demonstrates the preference of many individuals for deposits in financial inter-mediaries rather than direct market investments. These claims are usually insured and available in small denominations. They are also highly liquid, and the nominal principal value is impervious to cyclical changes in interest rates. The lower interest rates appear to be an acceptable price for reduced risks and the added convenience of time deposits.

Another drawback for many individual investors is the usual denomination of the municipal bonds. Many, if not most, taxpayers in the medium-to-high bracket have substantial incomes but rather modest accumulations of wealth. The standard denomination of municipal bond transactions ($5,000) does not permit these individuals to achieve adequate diversification through direct purchases of securities.

There have been intermittent efforts to appeal to small individual investors in municipal bonds; but the use of such devices as small-denomination bonds and direct sales has not

Table 10 Financial Asset Holdings of the Household Sector, Selected Years, 1950 to 1974

| Year | Total Financial Assets (Billions of Dollars) | Percentage Composition | | | | | |
		Municipal Securities	Corporate Equities	Demand Deposits and Currency	Savings and Time Deposits	U.S. Government Securities	Other Financial Assets*
1950	446.6	2.0	30.0	12.8	15.1	15.4	24.7
1960	972.8	3.2	40.9	7.6	17.0	7.6	23.7
1970	1,918.9	2.4	38.2	7.2	22.0	5.0	25.2
1974	2,182.6	2.8	24.0	8.0	31.9	5.5	27.8

*Includes corporate and foreign bonds, commercial paper, mortgages, life insurance and pension reserves, security credit, and miscellaneous assets.

Source: Board of Governors of the Federal Reserve System, *Flow of Funds Accounts* (various issues).

been highly productive. However, more hopeful results are being produced by a very different approach, namely, the development of municipal bond investment funds, called unit trusts. These provide diversification and are offered in convenient denominations (usually $1,000 but often much less). Initiated in 1961, unit investment trusts have grown from less than $20 million in outstanding assets to more than $6 billion at the end of 1975, when sales of shares in these funds were $2.5 billion.[22]

To enjoy a pass-through of the tax exemption to investors, these funds have been restricted to a specific portfolio of bonds that cannot be substantially altered throughout the life of the fund. The pass-through principle rests upon a 1961 Internal Revenue Service ruling that states that "*since under the proposed trust investment there is no power to reinvest in additional bonds or other securities or vary the investment in any manner*, the Tax-Exempt Public Bond Trust Fund, Series 1, will not constitute an association taxable as a corporation for federal income tax purposes."[23]

From the investor's point of view, the inability to reinvest the tax-exempt earnings from these funds automatically is both inconvenient and expensive. Moreover, the rigidities of the unit trust concept add to the risks and costs faced by underwriters, and these costs have to be passed on to investors in the form of higher-than-necessary sales charges.[24]

The rigidities imposed by the Internal Revenue Service have been circumvented by the very recent introduction of a new form of investment—the limited-partnership mutual fund. The first such fund—Kemper Municipal Bond Fund, Ltd.—was organized and introduced in May 1976.[25] Under the partnership form, income earned by this fund can flow through to investors without the imposition of a federal income tax. The Kemper Fund will operate as a managed, open-end mutual fund, with continuous offerings of shares (and a sales load of 4.25 percent on shares valued at less than $25,000), with redemptions (at net asset value), and with automatic dividend reinvestment. Moreover, as stated in its registration statement, the Kemper Fund will actively trade "principally to accomplish the Fund's objective in relation to anticipated movements in the general level of interest rates, but the Fund may engage to a limited extent in short-term trading consistent with its objective."[26] Fund shares will be offered at a $100 minimum initial investment.

Even though the device of the limited partnership appears to offer the flexibility of investment choice otherwise denied the corporate form of bond fund, it is cumbersome. Partnership agreements have to be updated and filed with the state in which the fund is organized, on a daily basis, and this requirement may create substantial overhead costs.

Because of the newness of the limited partnership, no firm forecasts of the potential demand for such funds can be made. Growth will be slowed, however, because new partnerships must be formed on a state-by-state basis and requi. e appropriate state legislative approval.

Of course, the most direct way to enable managed investment companies to compete for municipal bonds on behalf of their shareholders would be simply to amend the Internal Revenue Code. The mutual funds, public interest groups, and others are entreating Congress to pass such an amendment.[27]

Improving Market Efficiency

The outstanding characteristic of the municipal bond market is the large number and diversity of issuers and issues. During one week in July 1975, the same basic market mechanism was called upon to distribute both the massive $1 billion New York Municipal Assistance Corporation issue and the $20,000 School Building Bonds of Carrizozo, New Mexico. From 1970 through 1975, nearly 50,000 tax-exempt issues came to the marketplace—seven times the number of corporate issues handled during the same period (see Table 11). In 1975, over $58 billion in tax-exempt securities were marketed through 4,700 bond sales and 3,400 short-term note issues. This compares with about $50 billion in only 900 publicly underwritten corporate debt and equity issues during the same year.

The large number of issues and issuers means individual sales of relatively small size. Regardless of a trend toward larger offerings, tax-exempt security issues are still only one-fourth the size of average new corporate offerings.[1] Because of the structural characteristics of debt instruments, complexities are multiplied many times over. Most new issues are sold as serial bonds, and each issue may have as many as 30 different maturities and perhaps a dozen different coupon rates.[2] Of the 1 million different municipal securities now outstanding, no two are alike in maturity, coupon, issuer, credit rating, and yield.

Unlike the corporate market, until 1975 the tax-exempt

Table 11 Comparison of the Volume of New Issues in Municipal and Corporate Securities Markets, 1970 to 1975

(BILLIONS OF DOLLARS)

	Municipals						Corporate							
	Long-term		Short-term		Total		Bonds		Preferred Stock		Common Stock		Total	
Year	Num-ber	Vol-ume $	Num-ber	Vol-ume $	Num-ber	Vol-ume $	Num-ber	Vol-ume $	Num-ber	Vol-ume $	Num-ber	Vol-ume $	Num-ber	Vol-ume $
1970	4,701	17.8	2,903	17.9	7,604	35.6	549	24.3	55	1.3	778	5.5	1,382	31.1
1971	5,461	24.4	3,350	26.3	8,811	50.7	598	25.6	77	2.2	1,128	11.3	1,803	39.1
1972	5,103	22.9	3,317	25.2	8,420	48.2	469	18.9	78	2.3	1,383	13.0	1,930	34.2
1973	4,741	23.0	3,406	24.7	8,147	47.6	264	13.4	54	2.4	411	6.9	729	22.7
1974	4,287	22.8	3,414	29.0	7,701	51.9	376	27.3	57	1.7	154	2.6	587	31.6
1975	4,697	29.2	3,383	29.0	8,080	58.2	526	37.0	86	3.0	232	6.8	844	46.8

Note: Because of rounding, figures may not add up to totals.

Sources: "A Decade of Municipal Financing," *The Daily Bond Buyer,* January 7, 1976, p.5; "Total Underwritten Public Financing," *Investment Dealers Digest* (various issues).

market was not covered by the regulatory umbrella of the Securities and Exchange Commission. As a result, there had been little standardization of reporting practices in financial and other credit information furnished in sales documents accompanying new bond issues.[3] The dissemination of information is further hampered by the fact that most municipal bonds are sold as bearer bonds. Because the identity of the bondholders is not usually known, they do not receive unsolicited annual financial reports.

The large number of small issuers, the enormous supply of differing securities, and the lack of standard reporting systems have produced many variations in performance. Consequently, the municipal market falls well short of the competitive ideal of a homogeneous market. It is instead a richly textured aggregation of diverse local and national markets, the attributes of each depending upon the size and reputation of individual borrowers. Such fragmentation and heterogeneity can lead to additional marketing and distribution costs.

This, then, is the question: accepting the basic structure of the present market and the fundamental conditions of the supply and demand for tax-exempt securities, are the bonds designed, sold, and traded as efficiently and economically as possible? Accepted economic criteria can be used to judge the efficiency of this market. Generally, there are two broad measures: operating efficiency, which has to do with the cost structures of participants in the market, and allocative efficiency, which is achieved when prices are competitive and are the sole arbiters of how funds are used.[4] These provide a yardstick for measuring imperfections in the tax-exempt market and for analyzing existing or proposed correctives. In this chapter, we will examine the above question in terms of such technical features as the size of issues, trading practices, tax treatment, and the design and handling of issues.

DOES SIZE MATTER?

More than 70 percent of the *number* of general-obligation bonds sold in 1974 were for less than $2.5 million in par value (see Table 12). Only 2 percent of the general-obligation bond issues were $50 million or over. Nevertheless, this 2 percent soaked up 44 percent of the dollar volume of funds raised.

Revenue bonds tend to be much larger than general-obligation issues. Only half of the revenue issues were for less than $2.5 million in par value, while nearly 10 percent carried a face value of at least $25 million. The top 10 percent of revenue bond issues commanded well over half the investable funds; the smallest 12 percent attracted a minuscule four-tenths of 1 percent of the capital raised.

As in the corporate bond market, some large revenue bonds are sold as term bonds, of which the entire principal amount matures at one date (or a very limited number of dates) in the future. More common, however, are repayments scheduled as serial bonds, with portions of the principal maturing each year over a span running as long as 25 years. Combination serial and term issues are also used; there may be serial maturities for the first 10 years and a "balloon" amount maturing in, say, 30 years.[5]

Table 12   Percentage Distribution of Municipal Bond New Issues, by Size of Issue, 1974

Size of Issue (Millions of Dollars)	General Obligations (Percentage Distribution)		Revenue (Percentage Distribution)	
	Number of Issues	Total Dollar Amount	Number of Issues	Total Dollar Amount
Less than 0.5	34.4	1.7	12.2	0.4
0.5–1.0	16.9	2.7	11.9	1.0
1.0–2.5	21.3	7.5	25.8	4.3
2.5–5.0	13.0	10.1	17.9	7.1
5.0–10.0	7.9	12.0	12.7	9.9
10.0–25.0	3.5	11.8	10.7	18.4
25.0–50.0	1.3	10.0	5.2	19.9
Over 50.0	1.8	44.2	3.6	39.0

Source: Securities Industry Association data files.

Because of the serial payment structure, an issue already small by market standards is thus *further* subdivided into a set of individually smaller issues. A $5 million bond issue may have bonds maturing each year over a period as long as 25 years, with only $200,000 bonds maturing in any one year. In most instances, the $200,000 bonds coming due in 10 years are going to be treated as "different" securities from the $200,000 bonds maturing in the fifteenth or twentieth year, because interest rates for each maturity will be different, reflecting market preferences and expectations.[6]

The question is whether or not these small blocks of securities can be accommodated in a market that is concentrated more and more in large institutions. For the institutional investment manager, the larger the number of different securities owned, the greater the costs (clipping coupons, record keeping, and credit investigations) of maintaining a portfolio.[7] Moreover, certain costs borne by market intermediaries are fixed and are not dependent upon the size of a transaction. For example, sales effort and back-office operating costs are likely to be the same for an underwriter who sells a block of 2 or 200 bonds. Obviously, fixed costs will be proportionately larger for smaller transactions.

The marketplace imposes limitations, however, in the economies of scale that can be achieved through the size of a bond issue. Beyond a certain level, costs become larger for larger issues. This has been attributed to a weakness in "market digestion." Very large new issues, in addition to competing demands for capital, may require more funds than the market can commit comfortably. Because of the high level of risk to available underwriting capital in one offering, there is understandable pressure to price the bonds so that they sell quickly.[8]

Looked at another way, a very large issue conflicts with investors' efforts to reduce their risk by diversifying their portfolios. Increasing the supply of debt from any one issuer reduces the ability of the market to provide diversified portfolios. The new supply can be marketed only by compensating present and potential investors through higher returns.

Studies give equivocal answers to the question of what is the optimum size of issue. A study by Roland Robinson in 1960 suggested that the relationship between size and borrowing costs is likely to be "U-shaped." That is, very small issues will command slightly higher premium yields to offset the disproportionately high marketing costs. However, because of market congestion, very large issues may command higher interest rates than those of moderate size.[9]

More recent studies have found correlations between the number of bids submitted by underwriters and the interest cost. Reuben Kessel found that for small issues, there are fewer bids, underwriters require higher spreads, and the market demands higher reoffering yields.[10] Michael Hopwell and George Kaufman, using a large sample of bonds sold in the summer of 1973, suggest that the pattern of bidding follows an inverted U-shape: the peak in the number of bids occurs at approximately $12 million, with smaller and larger issues receiving fewer bids.[11]

Table 13 shows the relationship between the number of bids received and the size of the issue for all bonds offered through competitive bid in 1974. Small general-obligation bonds of less than $2.5 million in face value most often received only one bid, demonstrating that very small issues and issuers usually are restricted to local markets. Issues in the $2.5 million to $25 million bracket received four or more bids 60 percent of the time. Large issues of $50 million or more, however, attracted four or more bids in only one-third of sales. Revenue bonds generally attract even fewer bids when sold competitively. Small revenue issues in 1974 received more than one bid, and two-thirds of the very large revenue issues received no more than two bids.[12]

The number of underwriting bids is an important signal of the strength of market demand. By this standard, both very small and very large issues suffer from a relative lack of competitive market interest,[13] which causes higher borrowing costs.

Other important factors influencing borrowing costs are also correlated with the size of an issue. The relationship between issue size and credit ratings is depicted in Table 14.

Table 13   Percentage Distribution of the Number of Bids by Size of Issue for All Competitively Sold Municipal Bonds, 1974

Size of Issue (Millions of Dollars)	Percentage Distribution of the Number of Bids Received					
	1	2	3	4	5	6 or more
General-Obligation Bonds						
Less than 0.5	86.0	3.1	3.2	2.6	1.9	3.2
0.5–1.0	80.1	1.8	5.1	3.3	3.9	5.7
1.0–2.5	12.1	11.2	15.4	13.2	13.3	34.8
2.5–5.0	13.4	11.9	17.0	16.4	11.2	30.2
5.0–10.0	5.8	14.1	13.6	17.0	8.3	41.3
10.0–25.0	15.1	9.7	15.1	8.6	9.7	41.9
25.0–50.0	20.6	11.8	14.7	23.5	11.8	17.6
Over 50.0	6.7	15.6	42.2	13.3	8.9	13.3
Revenue Bonds						
Less than 0.5	98.0	1.0	0.0	1.0	0.0	0.0
0.5–1.0	95.5	2.2	1.1	0.0	1.1	0.0
1.0–2.5	27.1	18.9	19.5	17.5	6.4	10.5
2.5–5.0	36.1	22.3	7.3	12.3	12.3	9.7
5.0–10.0	17.4	23.3	23.3	18.8	11.5	5.8
10.0–25.0	19.1	14.9	14.9	27.7	12.8	10.6
25.0–50.0	12.5	29.2	41.7	4.2	12.5	0.0
Over 50.0	5.6	61.1	22.2	5.6	5.6	0.0

Source: Securities Industry Association data files.

Here, there is clearly an inverse relationship between the average size of the issue and the assigned rating. Small issues tend to have lower ratings or to be unrated, and this has important implications for the marketability of an issue. Any issuer seeking to command a national investor market must purchase a rating from at least one of the two major rating agencies. Once the bonds are sold, the need for information does not cease; situations change, investor needs and preferences change. The secondary market, where investors reshuffle outstanding securities, depends on a continuing flow of information so that values may be determined in light of current conditions and revised prospects.

Table 14   Relationship Between Municipal Bond Ratings and Average Issue Size, 1974

Moody's Ratings	General Obligations		Revenue	
	Number of Issues	Average Size (Millions of Dollars)	Number of Issues	Average Size (Millions of Dollars)
Aaa	231	13.13	27	15.85
Aa	583	6.00	158	10.27
A	1,313	4.33	588	9.65
Baa	399	1.98	189	6.78
Unrated	925	1.09	416	2.88

Source: Municipal Market Developments, February 28, 1975, Securities Industry Association, Economic Research Department.

The lack of readily available information, especially about the smaller issuer and its securities, has been a contributing factor in elevating the credit rating agencies as arbiters of credit quality. Without such ratings, investors would have to absorb the costs of compiling and analyzing the needed information themselves—an effort not worth the cost for small issues because of the low degree of credit risk that has prevailed in the market. The role of rating agencies is discussed in more detail in the next chapter.

CENTRALIZED BORROWING THROUGH STATE BOND BANKS

The municipal bond bank is a form of state credit assistance, addressing cost information and other problems faced by small borrowers in the tax-exempt market. The bank is a financial intermediary between the investment market and the local governments, the latter deciding whether to use the bond bank or sell their bonds independently. The mechanics are fairly simple. The bond bank issues notes or bonds in its own name and uses the proceeds to make loans to local governments. The bank's obligations are backed in the first instance by revenues from the constituent localities. The borrowings of these local units are general obligations and are accompanied by approving legal opinions from recognized bond counsel.[14] By presenting the capital market with a better "product" in a more economical package, the bond bank stimulates a broader national and institutional interest and thereby increases the supply of funds available to units that otherwise would be restricted to local or regional markets.

The bond bank concept came into being in December 1970, when the Vermont Municipal Bond Bank made its debut with a $4.6 million issue. The proceeds of this sale were used to purchase the obligations of 48 school districts and localities in Vermont. According to a study of the transaction, if these communities had sold individual bond issues on their own, they would have paid an additional $3 million in interest payments over the life of the obligations.[15] Since the initial offering in Vermont, similar bond banks have been set up in Maine and Puerto Rico, and other states have passed legislation authorizing their use.[16]

Perhaps the most compelling reason for the bond bank approach today is the market preoccupation with disclosure and reporting practices. The inexorable trend toward more complete, timely, and standardized reporting will very likely double or triple the costs of providing information on debt issues and financial conditions. Regardless of whether new standards emerge from federal regulation, market pressure, or voluntary action, the burden will fall most heavily on smaller jurisdictions already subject to built-in disadvantages in the market.

Centralized borrowing facilities can provide lower overhead costs. Certain of these costs (e.g., printing and advertising) loom larger for very small credits; a bond bank removes the necessity for contracting separately for these expenses. The overhead for the first Vermont issue was estimated to be half what it would have been if incurred under separate local sales.[17]

Bond banks can meet another need, that of supplying technical assistance to local government debt administration.[18]

They provide managerial aid to local financial officials who must muddle through the maze of financial details involved in debt issuance. For most smaller governmental units, a bond sale is a very occasional event that does not justify a permanent staff of financial and legal technicians. A centralized borrowing facility can maintain a professional staff and lower the overall costs of debt management for all localities. It can also provide the continuity and flexibility in debt management that most smaller units lack. Because of an inability to reach a broader market, many small borrowers have been forced to shorten their maturity structures and tailor offerings to the interests of local banks.[19] Moreover, small borrowers do not customarily have alternative sources of funds.[20] A centralized marketing agency has access to this broader market and can vary the timing and design of its bond issues.

By bundling smaller issues into one larger bond issue, the bond bank acts like a mutual fund. Purchasers of bond bank securities are, in effect, buying a diversified portfolio composed of a proportionate claim on each local borrower. A voluntary pooling arrangement of this sort is not likely to appeal to issuers who can command high credit ratings on their own merits. The bond bank, then, can be expected to carry a somewhat higher average risk of default on its portfolio.

As this suggests, success is determined by the commitment and the ability of the state to stand behind the debt of centralized borrowing authorities. Without state backing, potential investors would have to investigate each locality to establish their risk. This would clearly dissipate the gains of centralized marketing, as these costs would be passed on to borrowers in the form of higher interest rates, wider underwriting spreads, or fewer bids on new issues.

Several devices have been used to provide a form of superior overall credit, including (1) debt reserve fund, (2) a "moral commitment" by the state, (3) an outright state guarantee, (4) a state bond insurance fund, (5) modification of local finance laws to direct state aid to bond bank debt service prior to its distribution to the municipality, and (6) ad valorem taxing power for the bond bank itself. But the efficacy of any of these approaches depends upon the overall credit capacity of the state and its constituent units.

THE ROLE OF THE SECONDARY MARKET

Governments that sell securities are most concerned with the reception given a new debt issue in terms of the cost of credit and its availability. But investors have a broader perspective. In considering different investment opportunities, investors must evaluate the return on investments against perceived risks. Among the risks that are measured, market risk—the likelihood that an investment can be sold prior to maturity without significant loss in value—ranks high. The degree of risk can be evaluated by studying the performance of the secondary or trading market. A ready secondary market exists when the volume of the debt circulating in the market leads to a steady number of potential buyers. Efficient secondary markets, therefore, are important to all participants in the municipal funds market.

For investors, the ability to convert bonds into cash by sales in the secondary market prior to final maturity is an important determinant of liquidity. For intermediaries such as underwriters, brokers, and dealers, the breadth of the secondary market is a determinant of the risk involved in distributing a new issue. This risk is reflected in the gross profit (or spread) that they make from underwriting an issue and in the net interest cost to borrowers. For borrowers, an effective secondary market facilitates the issuance of securities with longer final maturities than would otherwise be possible. This protects borrowers against the uncertainties of future changes in interest rates and permits them to tailor the maturity of debt to the useful life of capital assets.[21]

The secondary market for tax-exempt securities is conducted almost entirely over the counter. Trading activities are not conducted on an organized central market exchange. As a consequence, individual transactions occur among dealers, brokers, and retail customers without a general dissemination of information on such details as price and volume traded.[22]

The over-the-counter nature of the secondary market and the lack of information about it make evaluation of its scope and functions difficult. But, essentially, there appear to be two secondary markets, one operating on a retail basis and the other as a wholesale system.

The secondary-market participation by small institutions and individual investors—the retail market—came under a cloud in recent years because of the fraudulent practices of a few unscrupulous dealers. Unsophisticated investors, exposed to the mind-boggling diffusion and heterogeneity of the tax-exempt market, proved to be particularly susceptible to such illegal practices as the misrepresentation of a defaulted revenue bond for a general obligation in good standing. Beginning in 1971, the Securities and Exchange Commission systematically began to crack down on shady operations:

> During that period, the Commission brought seven injunctive actions, involving over 72 defendants, to halt fraudulent municipal securities trading practices. Perusal of the Commission's complaints in these actions . . . reveals a disturbing pattern of professional misconduct by a significant number of broker-dealers.[23]

The regulatory framework legislated by the Congress in 1975 to combat such practices has yet to be defined completely. However, one clear mission of the newly formed Municipal Securities Rulemaking Board is to reverse the erosion in confidence that has been the inevitable result of the behavior of a limited number of unscrupulous "boiler room" operators. Their fraudulent schemes and the resulting publicity no doubt dampened the enthusiasm of small investors for the municipal bond market at a time when the market was under attack on other fronts.

By contrast, the professional or "wholesale" market, in which trades are conducted between dealers and brokers, appears to operate in a reasonably efficient manner. The most comprehensive source of data on this market is the *Blue List of Current Municipal Offerings,* a daily financial publication that carries a detailed record of bonds offered for sale by dealer firms and banks. An examination of the *Blue List* indicates that 700 to 900 securities dealers, including banks, participate actively in the secondary market, an apparent gain of some 100 to 200 firms since 1955.[24] The average daily volume of securities advertised for "bids wanted" in the *Blue List* in 1974 approached 9,000 issues with a face value of nearly $700 million. This compares with an average of 2,000 issues with a par value of $250 million in 1955.[25]

These statistics are only approximate indicators of the *change* in the secondary-market activity. A rule of thumb followed by market participants suggests that the actual transaction volume may be one or two times the size of the new issue market.[26]

On the assumption that the *Blue List* can be used as an index of the breadth of the secondary market, certain observations may be made. First, there tend to be proportionately more offerings of well-known issues and issuers than their share of outstanding debt would indicate.[27] This means that there is a more active market generally for the bonds of the larger and better-known borrowers. Second, trading in small lots in the market is costly. A study of the asking prices for securities advertised in the *Blue List* revealed that small blocks of bonds (less than $25,000) are offered at significantly lower prices (higher yields). But according to this study, economies of size diminish rapidly, and there are no systematic differences in asking prices for transactions of more than $200,000.[28]

A study has been made of actual transaction prices and yields for more than 1,000 dealer-to-dealer trades executed through a municipal bond broker during 1970 and 1971. These transactions took place under varying market conditions, and the securities analyzed carried different coupons, maturities, and ratings. The data indicated that more than three-fourths of the variations in yields and prices among these transactions could be explained by observed differences in maturity and credit risk. Although small trades usually commanded higher yields and lower prices, such transactions received nearly as many bids as larger trades. The average number of bids received on trades in the minimum denomination of $5,000 (one bond) was 6.2, while the average for all other trades was 8.8.[29]

These findings imply that, aside from the cost factors associated with size, there is a viable secondary market for small issues among professional dealers. Large issues or transactions reap some economies of scale, but over a wide range of transactions, such benefits are negligible. Other factors, such as perceived credit risks, have a greater impact on yields.

The role of the dealer is crucial in the operation of a viable secondary market. By maintaining positions in securities, the dealer provides the liquidity and continuity necessary to reduce the risks faced by investors who must sell their holdings prior to maturity. The ability and willingness of a dealer to maintain inventories depend upon the capital resources at his disposal and on the risks of future market developments.

In any securities market, dealers function with highly levered positions. That is to say, their equity capital commitment is small in comparison to the borrowing they do in order to finance their inventory of securities, which they pledge as collateral. Adverse market changes can thus lead quickly to insolvency. Such risks are exacerbated for tax-exempt dealers because of the unique characteristics of the municipal market.

In most securities markets, it is customary for dealers to take short positions (selling bonds that they do not own and that they must purchase in order to make delivery). This contributes to general market stabilization. But the lack of volume of securities with fixed attributes—coupon, maturity, and so on—creates substantial risks in holding such short positions, and municipal dealers always carry net long positions (actual ownership of bonds in inventory that have not been sold). The size of inventory and the interest costs of holding tax-exempt securities make dealers' profitability highly susceptible to unexpected and rapid increases in interest rates. When such increases occur, dealers must unload inventory as prices start to drop; these actions hasten the depreciation in bond prices and increase the volatility associated with municipal bonds.

WHY MUNICIPAL BONDS EXPERIENCE
GREAT PRICE VOLATILITY

Price volatility is a factor in all fixed-income securities because the prices of outstanding bonds are determined by the "current" level of yields on new issues. But in the case of municipal bonds, price volatility is exaggerated beyond that in other markets. This is basically due to fluctuations in demand, discussed in Chapter 4. In addition, there is even greater volatility in the secondary market because of the partially taxable nature of capital gains on tax-exempt bonds.

Because coupon rates of interest are fixed at the time a bond is issued, subsequent changes in overall market rates of interest are reflected solely through changes in the price of a previously issued bond. The purchaser of an outstanding bond selling at a price below its redemption, or par value, thus receives a coupon payment that is less than the current interest rate and—to make up the difference—a "capital gain." This capital gain is the difference between the purchase price and the par value of the bond at maturity.

The gain produces a tax effect that has significant consequences for the municipal market. Although the coupon portion of the total income stream remains tax-exempt, the capital gain portion is taxable—and is therefore less desirable. In other words, the return on any municipal bond bought at a price below par value becomes partially taxable.

The effect of depreciation in the prices of seasoned corporate and government securities is very nearly the reverse of what happens to the municipals. For many investors, the income on corporate and government securities in effect becomes partially tax-exempt because the capital gains are taxed at the *lower* capital gains rates. (This applies for all taxable investors except commercial banks.) The capital portion of income thus becomes more valuable than the coupon portion. This tends to lead to smaller changes in taxable bond prices than changes in new-issue reoffering yields suggest.[30]

The net effect of a given change in the market level of

interest rates on outstanding tax-exempt and taxable bonds, therefore, is asymmetrical. The partially taxable municipal bond fluctuates more in price than the partially tax-exempt corporate or government security.

TECHNICAL INNOVATIONS IN THE STRUCTURE AND SALE OF BONDS

Many proposals have been advanced to improve the design and sale of bonds and thus to lower the cost of long-term borrowing by state and local governments. Although these proposals generally require no new legislation, in some cases, minor changes would have to be made in state laws. A number of proposals are described in this section: the uses of alternative methods for measuring interest costs and determining winning bids, the use of term bonds, the adoption of floating rate bonds, and the option of extending or retracting maturities.

Alternative Methods of Awarding Bids   A large number of long-term tax-exempts now in the market already sell at prices below par and therefore carry the additional discount for the tax effect. Many bonds outstanding with more than 15 years to maturity were sold when interest rates were lower. However, a substantial volume of new issues sold each year are marketed *intentionally* with long-term bond maturities that are originally reoffered at discount prices.

The interest coupons placed on such maturities are often well below the prevailing market interest rate on instruments with similar maturities. Because part of the return on these bonds will be taxed as a capital gain, these issues must be priced to yield a higher return than if they carried coupons equal to current tax-exempt rates. Perhaps the most dramatic illustration of this practice is the state of Minnesota issue of September 1972. This was a 20-year serial bond issue for $25 million, sold with coupon rates of 0.1 percent—one-tenth of 1 percent —on bonds maturing from 1986 to 1992.

"Deep discount" bonds developed because of the present

system of calculating the interest cost on bond sales in order to determine the lowest bid. Unlike bonds in any other debt market, municipal bonds are typically sold on the basis of a simple interest concept called the net-interest cost method. The interest paid out by the issuer is given equal weight no matter when the payment is made, whether it is tomorrow or 40 years from now. But because a dollar of interest received tomorrow is of greater value to investors than interest received 40 years hence, the result of this practice is that bonds have a front-end load of interest and debt-service expenditures lump in the early years of a borrowing.

From a cost standpoint, the practice is inefficient. Borrowers' overall interest costs are increased because the resulting bonds typically must carry "penalty yields" to compensate investors either for the additional tax burden of discounted bonds or for the large premiums they pay for short bonds that carry high coupons.

From an analysis of this practice, the center for Capital Market Research at the University of Oregon has estimated that excess interest costs due to inefficient bond design may exceed $20 million over the entire life of all bonds issued in 1973.[31] The study concludes that these costly practices could be eliminated if issuers were to adopt present-value methods of calculating the interest cost of the bids submitted by underwriters, as is done in the other securities markets.

Term Bonds and Other Innovations   Several changes in the bond instrument have been suggested to enhance the appeal of distant-maturity obligations. One suggestion is to attempt to insulate investors from the potential price depreciation associated with purchasing-power risk and market risk. There are two variants to this approach.

One method is to issue long-term bonds with interest rates that change periodically, depending upon the level of rates on a suitable short-term money-market instrument. This was used in the debenture issues of several financial institutions in 1974. In practice, the interest on these "floating rate" bonds is generally pegged to the average Treasury bill rate over three- or six-month intervals.

A second method offers the investor the option of changing the maturity of his investment. There are two forms of optional or convertible maturity bonds—the "extendable" and the "retractable" options. The date to which the original maturity may be either lengthened or shortened (retracted) is established by the issuer at the time the bonds are sold.[32] There have been a number of these options offered in Canadian bond markets, but these are largely untested in the United States capital market.[33]

Floating rates and optional maturities are intended to cope with the perhaps disastrous effects of long-term inflation on fixed-rate long-term securities. But the usefulness of these devices is suspect. Ensuring the capital value of the bond does not remove the risk: it merely shifts it from investor to issuer. The governmental units that might have most need for such guarantees may also be the least likely to have the cash flow required to meet fluctuating debt-service payments implied in these instruments.

Greater use of conventional term bonds in place of the serial maturity structure could offer real advantages to the municipal borrower. Indeed, the term bond was formerly the common method of repaying municipal debt, and it continues to be the usual method for corporate securities and for many large tax-exempt revenue bonds. Because of the misappropriation by some issuers of sinking-fund money and the inability of others to manage these funds properly, the term bond came to be replaced by serial obligations for most governmental borrowers.[34]

If mandatory sinking funds are well handled, they provide a number of opportunities for flexible debt management. For example, when interest rates rise, the fund can be used to retire debt through purchases on the market at prices below their par value. When there are decreases in rates, the call feature can be used for early refunding of the entire issue, with substantial interest savings. Sinking funds also can be lenders of last resort, giving temporary relief in a hostile market and averting defaults, as happened in the New York crisis.

But this flexibility must be weighed against the most obvious drawbacks to the use of term bonds. The contractual obligation to pay interest at the generally higher rate attached to long-maturity instruments is one such drawback. And there is also the need—and it cannot be overstressed—for skilled government financial managers.

8

Better Credit Information and Greater Disclosure

In order for a market to allocate resources efficiently, all participants must have equal and ready access to the information required to decide upon an investment. This general principle applies to any market. To raise capital on most favorable terms, issuers of municipal bonds need to know the attitudes and preferences of investors. Investors, who are purchasing a claim on the future revenues of borrowers, must have information that enables them to estimate the certainty of receiving promised payments.[1] Because of the multiplicity of issues and issuers, the municipal market poses particularly severe problems for assembling information, with resulting imperfections in the marketing and trading processes.

The demand for adequate credit information is among the most pressing issues in the municipal market. The rush of events in 1974 and 1975 shook investor confidence in the market and focused attention on the question of disclosure. Amid the alarms of impending default and catastrophic bankruptcy, investors developed doubts about the protection of the familiar statement found in prospectuses promising that "the full faith and credit of this government are pledged to the payment of principal and interest on these bonds and the government is obligated to levy *ad valorem* taxes without limitations as to rate or amount upon all the taxable property, sufficient to pay the principal of and interest on the bonds."

Comforting words, perhaps, but would borrowers live up to them? Were governments telling the investors all they needed to know, not only to avoid potential defaults but to gauge properly the full risks of owning a security? And, above all, what were the legal liabilities of those selling the bonds—what information was needed and who was responsible for it?

As the market became sensitive to the subject, Ohio, New Jersey, and various large local governments experienced well-publicized difficulties in marketing bonds because of alleged disclosure problems. People suddenly became interested in how governments keep their books, securities attorneys discovered a virgin territory for their arcane skills, and legislators began to reexamine the duties and powers of the states to monitor and oversee the finances of their local subdivisions. Perhaps the most far-reaching consequence of the debacle that began in New York was the unmistakable movement toward making available much more and better information about government finances, a reform that would benefit investor and taxpayer alike.

CREDIT RATINGS

The extent and diversity of the municipal bond market have given rise to professional services that specialize in judging and disseminating information about the creditworthiness of borrowers. The two national bond rating agencies, Moody's and Standard & Poor, are the dominant information brokers in the tax-exempt market because they supply information and analysis at a low price compared to the cost of developing alternative information systems.[2]

The rating attached to a bond has become more than an advisory opinion on the relative creditworthiness of a security. It is accepted as a standard of value that, within a range, indicates the cost of borrowing to a municipality. Because of its great importance to the market, the rating, as a prime determinant of price, has taken on something of a life of its own, including its own elements of risk.[3] At the same time, ratings have become tools of financial regulation used to influence portfolio structure, to evaluate bank liquidity and capital adequacy, and to determine eligible forms of collateral.[4]

It is clear, of course, that the capital market looks beyond credit ratings when evaluating tax-exempt issues. The variation of interest costs for bonds within a specific rating class is an obvious example. Daniel Rubinfeld, attempting to discriminate between the rating effect and an independent "market effect," concludes that

> published ratings do have an effect on market yields which is independent of the market's evaluation of the community's financial situation. However, at most 34 of the 80 basis points between AAA and BAA yields can be explained by the credit rating itself. The remainder of the spread is due in part to varying market conditions at the time of offer and to the market evaluation of the communities.[5]

The degree to which market evaluation is dependent upon ratings is a cause of considerable concern. The rating process is imprecise. Although many variables held to be important are enumerated, there is no widely disseminated formula that defines how, why, or to what degree certain factors enter into a specific rating. Nor is there disclosure of the relative weights assigned to the characteristics used in rating securities. Such ambiguity keeps investors and regulatory authorities from evaluating the majority of bonds that are unrated in a manner consistent with the evaluation of rated bonds. It fails to provide specific guidelines by which communities can try to raise a low rating.[6]

These ambiguities were examined in the 1974 study of credit rating systems sponsored by the Twentieth Century Fund. The background paper prepared for that study stated that the rating agencies

> have never revealed exactly why they think New York City has the same credit risk as Pascagoula, Mississippi, or why they think Rochester, New York, should stand two rungs higher on the scale of credit quality than either one. Is the Stamford Parking Authority really "high quality by all standards" and the New Jersey Educational

Facilities Authority merely "lower medium grade"? Perhaps these were valid distinctions, but only the credit rating agencies know how they were determined.[7]

In reporting its findings, the Twentieth Century Fund Task Force on Municipal Bond Credit Ratings did not dispute the appropriateness and usefulness of private opinions about public credit. But it did express reservations about the market's dependence on the agencies' summary rankings and the paucity of more basic credit information and competing opinions. The Task Force recommended a series of actions at both the state and federal levels.[8] The most important and far-reaching recommendation was that a national data bank should be created to collect and distribute credit data about state and local borrowers. The data bank should not be designed to provide credit judgments of its own. Its purpose should be to conduct research, undertake programs to improve the general quality and comparability of information, and provide a national information network. The Task Force favored a network backed by a nonprofit joint effort of municipal market participants, not by a government agency.[9]

REPORTING PRACTICES OF ISSUERS

The financial reporting practices of state and local governments—an area that has been largely overlooked by issuer and investor—have not been the subject of much systematic study. The work done to date has found that reporting reflects the differing characteristics of local governments. Reporting is typically geared not to informing the investor but to meeting state requirements that stress the legality of a government's affairs, not its financial health. Neglecting the latter has not been without its costs. In its study of financial emergencies in American cities, the Advisory Commission on Intergovernmental Relations (ACIR) concluded that accounting and reporting practices of state and local governments were generally of poor quality. ACIR said that "as a consequence of inadequate accounting and reporting, some cities have drifted into financial emergencies without realizing how serious their problems have become."[10]

A recent study by the Municipal Finance Study Group has been directed more specifically at the documents—variously called official offering statements, reports of essential facts, or prospectuses—that accompanied a large sample of general-obligation bond issues sold during the last four months of 1975.[11] The bond issues in the survey range from a small $900,000 issue sold by a Midwestern city to several $50 million issues sold by states. The offering statements were analyzed to determine whether or not sufficient information was provided to enable an experienced credit analyst to investigate credit strengths and weaknesses.[12]

The survey, taken just before the great disclosure scare of 1975, found a wide range of reporting practices and frequent omissions of items that were pertinent to a full description of both the borrowers and the securities. Although most offering statements provided a comprehensive statement of currently outstanding debt, more than 90 percent omitted any record of past debt, and 80 percent omitted a detailed schedule of annual future debt service. Only 7 of the 174 statements contained audited financial reports, and only 25 incorporated detailed operating statements of revenues and expenditures. Most of the official statements did not furnish detailed statistics on the economic base and demographic characteristics of the issuer.[13]

These studies confirm the widely held view that the amount of information disclosed by issuers has been generally sparse. But until recently, little pressure has been brought to bear on borrowers to make fuller disclosure. As the ACIR observed in 1973:

> Progress in improving municipal accounting and reporting is slow because of the lack of incentives for improvements. Investors who would not consider investing their money in a corporation that failed to have an independently audited annual financial report conforming to the nationally accepted standards for private accounting and reporting readily invest in municipal bonds without benefit of such a report.[14]

Present-day reporting practices are the vestiges of a time when defaults were not only rare but unthinkable, and the benefits of more facts and better analysis were far outweighed by the costs of gathering and disseminating such information.

CREDIT RISK IN MUNICIPAL BONDS

Municipal bonds commonly have been regarded as having extremely high credit quality. Timely payment of principal and interest is given heavy emphasis by bond salesmen as a reason for investing in municipals. The most widely used primer on the municipal bond industry, *Fundamentals of Municipal Bonds*, states that "the security of such bonds is generally considered to be second only to the bonds of the United States Government."[15] Such assurances have been founded on a 40-year absence of defaults and losses from defaults in municipal bonds. One must go back to the 1930s to find widespread state and local government delays in making payments on their debt obligations.

It has been estimated that for the period from 1929 through 1937, approximately $1.4 billion in state and local interest and principal went into default at various times. This equaled slightly more than 7 percent of the total state and local debt outstanding in the early 1930s.[16] By comparison, approximately $4.5 billion in corporate bonds defaulted over the same interval, equaling approximately 20 percent of the average outstanding long-term corporate debt during the early 1930s. By 1944, there remained some $3 billion outstanding in defaulted corporate bonds, whereas past-due interest and principal on municipals did not much exceed $100 million at the end of the 1930s.[17]

Difficulties in state and local government debt-service payments have been minimal during the long period of prosperity since World War II. There were 431 recorded instances of late or defaulted payments from 1945 through 1969, of which more than 300 were evidently of a technical or temporary nature.[18] Nearly all of the defaulted securities were held locally (96 percent of the payment difficulties involved

holdings of banks in the same city or state as the bond issuer).
Defaults in the postwar period have shown no cyclical pattern;
they have simply reflected the increase in the total number of
issues outstanding.

It has been estimated that the permanent loss of principal and interest amounted to less than $10 million (1/10,000
of the debt outstanding) at the end of 1965.[19] The total dollar
volume of defaulted municipal bonds over the entire 30-year
period from 1945 through 1974 is estimated at $500 million
(of which $334 million represented three large toll-revenue
bond issues). This was about 0.25 percent of all municipal
bonds outstanding as of the beginning of 1975.[20]

Continuing the comparison of municipal and corporate
defaults, recent experience again demonstrates that, until the
note moratorium of New York City, municipal securities maintained a superior record of payment. In the 1970s, the collapse of the Penn Central and other major defaults led to an
estimated $1.3 billion of defaults in corporate long-term
securities; in addition, approximately $300 million in short-
term paper defaulted. Until the end of 1975, there was no
comparable experience in the municipal securities market. Except for its devastating influence on investor confidence, even
the $100 million, 96-day default in New York Urban Develop-
ment Corporation notes was a relatively minor lapse. However, the moratorium on the $1.6 billion in New York City
notes in December 1975, although technically a forced exchange, is generally considered a major default. Although it is
difficult to compare the postponement of short-term debt repayments with that of long-term bonds, the New York moratorium makes it clear that the long-standing safety record of
municipal bonds has been seriously flawed.

CREDIT QUALITY AND INTEREST COSTS

The effect of sustained tranquillity in the municipal bond
market was reflected in the trend of interest rates on municipal
securities relative to similarly rated corporate debt securities.
Chart 2 traces the interest rate movements on the lowest-

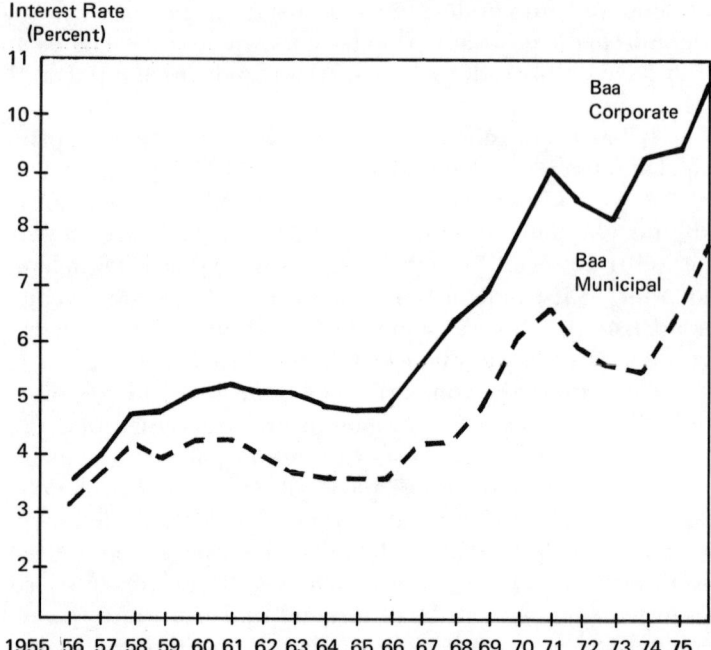

Interest Rate
(Percent)

Source: Moody's Investor Service.

Chart 2   Average Annual Interest Rates on Long-term Municipal and Corporate Bonds Rated Baa

investment-grade bonds (carrying Baa ratings from Moody's). This chart demonstrates that the difference in interest rates widened considerably from 1955 to 1974. From 1955 to 1960, the Baa municipal interest rate averaged 86 percent of the comparable corporate bond rate, and this dropped to only 68 percent for the period from 1970 to 1974. By the same token, interest rate differentials in the municipal market narrowed (see Chart 3). The Baa rate on municipals was 65 percent of the Aaa rate between 1955 and 1960; it was 90 percent between 1970 and 1974.

This long-term trend completely reversed itself in 1974 as interest rates on the lowest-investment-grade municipal bonds rose sharply, relative to the corporate bond rate. During 1975, the ratio of tax-exempt to taxable interest rates on

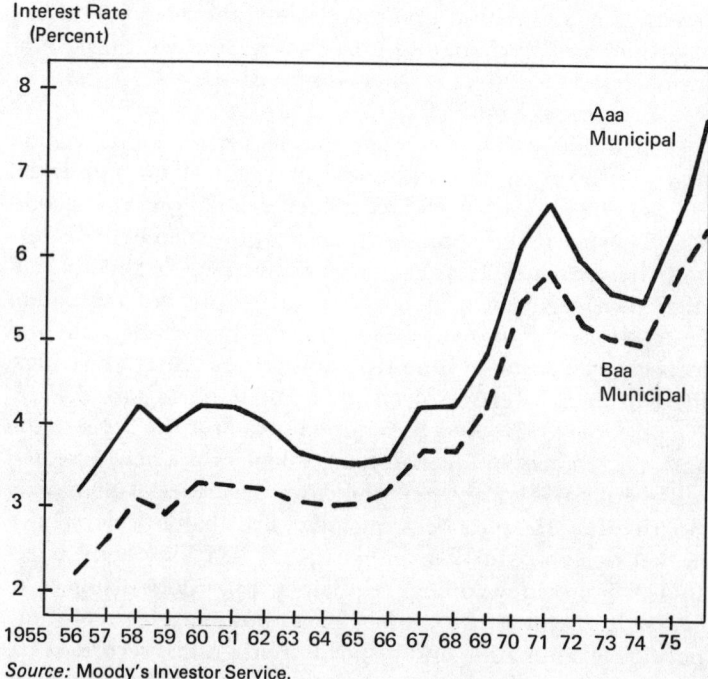

Interest Rate
(Percent)

Aaa
Municipal

Baa
Municipal

1955 56 57 58 59 60 61 62 63 64 65 66 67 68 69 70 71 72 73 74 75

Source: Moody's Investor Service.

Chart 3   Average Annual Interest Rates on Municipal Bonds Rated Aaa and Baa

Baa-rated bonds climbed from 67 percent in February to 78 percent in November. Likewise, as investors increasingly distinguished among credit strengths within the municipal market, differences in yields between bonds carrying the highest and lowest investment-grade ratings almost doubled between January and December of 1975.

MUNICIPAL BOND REGULATION AND DISCLOSURE

A significant development was the passage of the Securities Acts Amendments of 1975, which extended regulation to the municipal bond market under the federal securities laws. Prior to this, brokers and dealers doing business solely in municipal securities were not subject to regulations by any agency of the federal government. Because of the fraudulent practices of some unscrupulous dealers, the attention of the Securities and Exchange Commission was drawn to the municipal bond secondary market in the early 1970s.

Bringing the municipal market into regulation presented special problems. The first was to devise a system of regulation that would reflect the traditional practices of the municipal market; the industry itself favored self-regulation. The second was to ensure that the same regulations governed both dealers and the securities transactions of banks (which already had their own regulators). The third was to prevent regulation from impairing the vital capital-raising powers of state and local governments. In June 1975, after three years of hearings, these problems were resolved and legislation was passed.[21]

The Securities Acts Amendments call for the registration and regulation of municipal security dealers by a newly created self-regulatory body, the Municipal Securities Rulemaking Board. Its 15 members include five bank-dealers, five broker-dealers, and five public members. This body is responsible for developing regulatory provisions, subject to oversight by the SEC.[22] It has broad powers for establishing periodic examination and inspection programs, record-keeping requirements, and rules to ensure fair market practices. Although the board is essentially an industry self-regulatory body with the power to adopt binding rules, the SEC retains the ultimate authority to delete, change, or compel adoption of new rules.

State and local governmental issuers retain their historic exemptions from the registration requirements of the Securities Act of 1933 and from the reporting requirements of the Securities and Exchange Act of 1934. Under amendments to the 1934 law, neither the SEC nor the board can require an issuer to file information prior to the sale of its municipal securities. Nor can they require an issuer to furnish information on itself, either directly or indirectly through a municipal securities dealer or otherwise.[23] Nevertheless, despite this, the antifraud provisions of the federal securities laws apply to all participants in transactions in municipal securities.[24] And although the extent of their liability is untested, issuers evidently have an obligation under the federal securities laws not to misstate or omit material information.[25]

The rush of events in 1975 rapidly drove the tax-exempt markets into a thicket of disclosure problems. In the wake of the UDC note default in March and the chaotic market condition of New York City bonds, there were charges of fraud on the part of underwriters and politicians. Municipal bond dealers, worried about the gathering clouds of liability under the antifraud statutes, began to believe that control of credit information might be needed.[26]

As yet, there seems to be no clear direction to the debate. Although many have called for some regulation of information provided by issuers, there is little agreement on how it is to be accomplished.[27] One approach proposes either the registration of municipal securities under the Securities Act of 1933 or the repeal of the 1934 act's exemptions in order to permit regulation of issuer information either by the rulemaking board or by the SEC directly.[28] Another proposal, the subject of congressional hearings in early 1975, would require standardized new issue information and current reporting for municipal bond issues and issuers above certain sizes.[29] Another possibility would be to create a new and specialized regulatory body, made up of issuers, to deal with governmental disclosure problems.[30] Or registration might be put on a voluntary basis for those governments that feel the market for their securities would thereby be improved.[31]

Others argue that in the absence of a regulatory mechanism, the main discipline should be provided by the market and reinforced by state laws. Standards of disclosure and investigative procedures should be developed by underwriters and others in order to protect investors when they buy municipal securities.[32] Publication of suggested disclosure guidelines by the Municipal Finance Officers Association (MFOA) was an early step in this direction.[33] A bill establishing comprehensive local government disclosure requirements, modeled after the MFOA guidelines, has been filed in New York State, and several other states are preparing to move in the same direction.[34]

Although this is undoubtedly only a beginning, investors already have an important lever (which has been overlooked until now) for prying information from issuers—the antifraud provisions. After years on the fringes of regulation, dealers and governments suddenly found themselves having to grasp the new and elusive concept of disclosure. Their ability to devise standards and procedures that will be observed widely is of paramount importance.

EXPANDING THE STATE ROLE

The devastating effects of the events of 1975 quickened interest in the role of the states in preventing fiscal disasters among their local governments and agencies. State governments obviously play a pivotal role in most areas that need improvement—accounting and reporting systems, disclosure procedures, and designing and marketing of debt sales. State legislatures and agencies have the power to establish the laws, regulations, and centralized services that will make reforms legally required and operationally possible.

Although the painful object lessons of laxity in these matters are relatively new, the call for greater state involvement is not. In 1965, the Advisory Commission on Intergovernmental Relations undertook a comprehensive study of state aids to local government debt administration and generally found that there was an overemphasis on often antiquated legal restrictions and a lack of technical help.[35] Eight years later, the commission, in its study of financial emergencies, again urged the states to take positive steps to improve financial information and management capabilities and to monitor local government fiscal conditions.[36] These recommendations were underscored by the Twentieth Century Fund Task Force on Municipal Credit Ratings, which concluded that "at a minimum, . . . every State should make available timely, uniform, consolidated financial reports and sponsor technical assistance in local debt management and promote its use."[37]

The first step—and the most difficult—in correcting the situation is to find out what is going on. A large part of the information problem appears to be that many states are microcosms of the diffusion of responsibility and the network of requirements that bewilder observers on the national scene. Although reams of information bearing on financial condition are collected, as a rule, little of it is geared to marketing bonds or reporting to investors. Furthermore, data are gathered by a host of audit agencies, budget offices, planning groups, and community affairs operations, and all of these data are seldom available from a single source. Moreover, when information is published, it is often in summary form and several years late.[38]

Once data are assembled, the next ordeal is to understand what they mean. Governments do not keep books the same way that business enterprises do.[39] There are generally accepted governmental accounting principles. But here, again, the orientation has been toward legal compliance—meeting state laws, which not only vary from state to state but frequently do not conform to accepted accounting principles.[40] In such circumstances, it is vital to analysis that the differences be explained. But not all states require an audit of local government financial reports, and even fewer demand that audits be done in conformance with generally accepted principles.[41] Obviously, the first, and perhaps most difficult, steps to be taken are toward greater uniformity and timeliness in governmental accounting and reporting. At present, the principal inspiration to achieving these goals is the demands of wary investors.

Several states have a battery of technical assistance programs to improve local government financial management, but only a few have put together a major, consolidated effort to meet the specialized needs of debt management. The leading example is the North Carolina Local Government Commission, which not only offers a broad range of technical services but also has the power to approve bonds before they are marketed.[42] Other states, though not as ambitious as the North Carolina model, have established debt advisory agencies that monitor local government conditions, report on their activities, and, upon request, provide technical services.[43] Studies of the effects of these activities indicate that the market both notices and appreciates the differences and that the relatively modest expenditures are recouped in lower borrowing costs.[44] However, it remains to be seen whether the states, seemingly dedicated to devising more uses for the tax-exempt bond, are at last being induced to ensure that such bonds are marketed in a reasonably fair and efficient manner.

9

Policies and Programs to Strengthen the Municipal Bond Market

Some improvements in the operation of the existing municipal bond market can be made without altering the basic structure of the market, but because that structure has weaknesses, more fundamental changes may be required. The tax-exempt subsidy on which the market relies is the basis of infirmities, for not only is tax exemption inefficient as a subsidy, but, from the federal tax collector's point of view, it is inequitable as well. It is also a basic cause of the fluctuating investment demand that makes the market so unsettling and exceedingly expensive for those caught at the top of the swing.

The volatility of the market and its great reliance on the tax subsidy have resulted in many suggestions for improvement. These range from ways to make it easier to sell tax-exempt bonds to proposals for replacing tax-exempts with taxable securities. Although each proposal follows a different course, each has the same objective: to reduce the level and the volatility of borrowing costs for state and local governments. The proposals fall into a number of broad categories: direct interest subsidies, insurance and guarantees, secondary-market support programs, changes in federal tax treatment, removal of constraints on competition, mandated or induced investments, and greater restraints on the uses of tax-exempt borrowing. (This chapter describes the mechanics of the leading proposals. The appendix following this chapter discusses the operation of the proposals in terms of the demand-and-supply analysis so often used by economists.)

DIRECT INTEREST SUBSIDIES

Certain policy options are designed to separate the cost of borrowing to the state or local government from the yield or return to lenders by introducing explicit and direct interest subsidies. As a group, these proposals assume that investor demand for tax-exempt bonds either is insensitive to relative rates of interest or is too limited or volatile to match the supply of such debt at reasonable and stable rates of interest. In other words, they assume that the market is weak. The textbook definition of a "weak" market involves such complexities as elasticities of demand and investor surpluses. Put simply, the net effect is that the gap narrows between rates of interest on tax-exempt and taxable securities, thus cutting down on the value of the tax-exempt privilege.

Earlier chapters traced both cyclical and secular pressures in the municipal market to its reliance on a limited number of institutional and individual investors with equally limited appetites for long-term, tax-exempt securities. Some communities are always faced with high borrowing costs, and all communities pay high rates during periods of tight credit. Whatever the underlying causes, high borrowing costs dilute the value of the tax-exempt subsidy, aggravate tax burdens, and may even drive some borrowers out of the market. A rise in tax-exempt rates relative to taxable interest rates induces inequities in a system of progressive income taxes and produces losses in revenue to the federal government.

One way to alleviate this situation is to broaden the market by tapping the vast pool of institutional funds held by insurance companies, pension funds, and thrift institutions. These investors have long-term and predictable liabilities and a proclivity for investing in long-term, fixed-income securities. But because they are either exempt from taxation or in relatively low marginal tax brackets, they have little reason to accept the lower yields that typify tax-exempt securities. To attract this group, state and local governments would have to increase the returns on their securities to a level competitive with market yields on taxable securities.

One approach would facilitate this by introducing an interest subsidy, sometimes referred to as an "interest wedge." The interest subsidy makes up the difference between tax-exempt and taxable interest rates. State and local governments would borrow at the lower rate, but investors would receive the higher yields that are demanded on taxable securities. Proposals differ on how this wedge will be set up. These differences involve marketing technicalities, administrative measures, and the scope of eligibility. But the basic mechanism and intended effects are similar[1] and can best be demonstrated through a review of the most popular subsidy proposal—the taxable bond option.

TAXABLE BOND OPTION

Fundamentally, the taxable bond option (TBO) calls for the federal government to pay some proportion of the annual interest expenses incurred by those state and local units that choose to issue their bonds on a taxable rather than a tax-exempt basis. In its long history,[2] there have been many variants of the TBO.

In the least complicated version, state and local governments would retain full control over the timing, amount, and purposes of their debt financing, and, in addition, they would have the option of receiving bids for new issues as *either* taxable *or* tax-exempt. The federal government, through a permanent appropriation, would contract to pay a fixed percentage of the interest cost of those bonds sold on a taxable basis. State and local governments would select the bid that resulted in the lowest effective interest cost.

By making this optional method of sale possible, the subsidy should bring about various changes in interest rates and investment patterns. On the assumption that the option is freely and generally available, the key determinants of its uses and benefits are the level of the subsidy and bond market conditions. The subsidy is generally expressed in terms of the percentage of the taxable interest rate, and specific subsidy proposals range from 30 to 50 percent.[3]

As noted in Chapter 4, a plan to provide state housing finance agencies with a taxable bond option at a 33 1/3 percent subsidy rate is being implemented by the Department of Housing and Urban Development. Using this rate as an example, the TBO would establish a ceiling on the ratio of tax-exempt to taxable rates for otherwise comparable housing bonds. Specifically, if interest rates on taxable bonds were at 9 percent and tax-exempt rates at 6.5 percent, housing agencies would find it in their best interest to issue taxable bonds; their net interest cost after the one-third subsidy would be only 6 percent. If the option were generally available to all municipal issuers, then as long as savings were possible borrowers would continue to choose the TBO. Transferring sales to the taxable market in this way reduces the supply of tax-exempt securities and results in lower tax-exempt interest rates. Through this process, tax-exempt rates would fall to 6 percent, or two-thirds of the taxable interest rate. At that point, the issuers would sell bonds in either market, depending upon which presented the most favorable conditions at the time of sale. As this example suggests, the higher the subsidy rate, the greater the inducement for municipalities to select the taxable bond option.

Some critics of the TBO have feared that a high rate of subsidy will raise interest rates in the taxable bond market because of the increase in taxable municipal issues. If this occurs, they point out, traditional issuers of taxable securities (private corporations and the federal government) will be penalized. Moreover, the upsurge in taxable rates would reduce the usefulness of the TBO to governmental issuers. However, estimates of the impact, based on large-scale and sophisticated econometric models, suggest that the increase in taxable rates with a 40 percent interest subsidy would be on the order of 10 to 15 basis points.[4] Thus, if taxable rates were 9 percent, tax-exempt rates were 6.3 percent, and a taxable bond with a 40 percent subsidy rate were introduced, taxable rates might rise to 9.15 percent, but tax-exempt rates would fall to 5.5 percent. The small increase in taxable rates and the much larger decrease in tax-exempt rates reflect the fact that the market for taxable securities is much broader than the tax-exempt market.

During the past decade, the ratio of tax-exempt to taxable bond yields for comparable 20-year bonds has averaged about 70 percent. Therefore, a subsidy rate would have to exceed 30 percent to cause a significant number of municipal borrowers to choose the taxable bond alternative on a fairly regular basis. (A continuing flow of such bonds is seen by some as important in creating a stable market for them.) If the federal subsidy rate were set considerably higher—say, approaching 50 percent—virtually all municipal borrowers would choose the taxable option, and new issue long-term tax-exempt bonds would disappear. This would greatly lower the cost of state and local borrowing and would represent an enormous subsidy to borrowing.[5] But it also would undermine the tax-exempt borrowing privilege and make borrowers dependent on federal government subsidies to support their borrowing. Therefore, most proposals have entailed subsidy rates high enough to attract a significant number of municipal borrowers but not so high as to effectively eliminate the tax-exempt market.

With a fixed rate of subsidy, the TBO would be of greatest benefit in times of tight money. In a period of easy credit, for example, at a fixed subsidy rate of 33 1/3 percent and with new issues of $25 billion per year, an estimated $2.5 billion, or 10 percent of the total offerings, would be in taxable securities. But in periods of tight credit, roughly 20 percent of the market—about $5 billion in bonds—would move to the taxable market.[6] Use of the TBO as such an overflow device would prevent tax-exempt yields from rising to more than two-thirds of comparable taxable yields in periods of tight credit.

The cost-benefit relationship of the interest subsidies must be examined from the federal view. The Treasury estimates that increased federal tax revenues resulting from the substitution of taxable for tax-exempt bonds would offset federal subsidies to the 30 percent subsidy level. However, as the subsidy rate increases above that level, net federal costs (excess of subsidy payments over increased tax revenues) can become substantial.[7] But most estimates agree that the total reduction in borrowing costs to state and local governments would be many times greater than the net cost of the plan to the Treasury.[8]

The taxable bond option reported by the House Ways and Means Committee in the spring of 1976 contained many provisions designed to minimize the administrative requirements of the program. Issuers would be free to take bids for bonds on both a tax-exempt and taxable basis, and the subsidy would be remitted directly to the paying agent and released only after the issuer had deposited his share of the interest payment. Although the option would be available to all types of obligations that are now tax-exempt, the Ways and Means version specifically excluded its use for industrial revenue bonds and issues receiving other forms of direct federal credit assistance. Furthermore, the option could not be used if the taxable bonds were held by a related governmental agency unless they had been sold competitively in a public underwriting. The bill would establish a 35 percent subsidy rate to be funded by entitlement to a permanent authorization.[9]

The taxable bond option has several advantages over other forms of direct interest subsidy. It minimizes federal intervention and control in marketing state and local debt. It is both permissive and inclusive: knowing the subsidy rate, state and local borrowers may decide whether or not to use the taxable bond option. Furthermore, the private capital market continues to exercise its collective judgment and can distinguish among individual credits.

Support for the taxable bond option concept has been mixed since the original proposal in 1969. Among the state and local governmental groups, attitudes range from the warm support now given to the idea by the National League of Cities and the National Conference of Mayors to the chilling opposition of the Association of State Auditors, Treasurers, and Comptrollers. In recent testimony, the Securities Industry Association, which has alternately opposed and supported the option, landed somewhere in the middle and conceded that the TBO was the least undesirable means of federal assistance to the municipal market.[10] The major difficulties with the TBO continue to be fears about the potential power of a direct subsidy to dictate the terms of state and local borrowing and a basic disagreement over whether or not such an option would be consistent with the preservation of the tax-exempt bond market. That debate—and both sides are ardently represented in any discussions—has both economic and political dimensions and continues to defy resolution.[11] The option will probably be used experimentally on a program-by-program basis, and its success or failure here will determine its future as an alternative for the general market.

FEDERAL FINANCING AUTHORITIES

In July 1968, then Vice-President Hubert Humphrey advocated the creation of a National Urban Development Bank to help finance the needs of American cities. Developed more fully by the President's Task Force on Urban Problems, an Urban Development Bank (Urbank) was recommended in the *Economic Report of the President* in January 1969 and introduced in the Senate by Senator John Sparkman the same month.

Urbank would be authorized by the federal government and owned by states, localities, and private investors, who would buy capital stock in the corporation. Funds would be raised in the taxable market and reloaned by the federal financing authority at below-market rates of interest to eligible governments that could not be accommodated "reasonably" in the tax-exempt market. The interest subsidy would be set high enough, or the relending rate low enough, to reduce the volume of tax-exempt securities. Consequently, demand for the remaining supply of tax-exempts would lower the cost, thus improving the efficiency of the indirect subsidy granted through tax exemption. The losses—the difference between Urbank's borrowing rate and its lending rate—would be made up by automatic transfers from the federal Treasury, but the additional taxes collected on the taxable securities would offset a large share of the cost. The logic here, of course, is identical to that found in the TBO.[12]

The Environmental Financing Authority (EFA), enacted

into law in 1972 but never made operational, has a similar design. The EFA would function as a federal intermediary to finance the nonfederal share of waste-treatment construction projects, borrowing in the taxable market and purchasing obligations of states and localities at preferential rates of interest. In a review of the proposal, the Advisory Commission on Intergovernmental Relations endorsed a pilot "test [of] the ability of a Federally subsidized lending operation to broaden state and local access to the capital market."[13] Although borrowing only for specific purposes, the EFA, in common with Urbank, would interpose a federal intermediary between state and local borrowers and the capital market.

Mechanisms such as Urbank have not generally survived the rigors of political debate, and questions remain regarding the definition and workability of eligibility standards, the need for federal inspection of financial practices, the control over the level of the interest subsidy, and the exercise of these controls to conform with national economic policy. Moreover, state and local governments have expressed concern that hard-dollar grants would be replaced by "soft" loans or guarantees—in other words, that federal credit assistance would become a substitute for grants.

Direct Subsidies to Selected Tax-Exempt Investors   Giving inducements to selected purchasers of tax-exempt securities in the form of interest subsidy payments is another suggested means of attracting more investable funds into the municipal market. Certain tax-exempt institutional investors could be subsidized to hold municipal bonds—in effect, keeping these bonds out of the hands of those who would use them as tax shelters.

An Urban Institute proposal provides for interest subsidy payments to governmental retirement funds and unemployment trust funds that elect to purchase tax-exempt bonds.[14] State and local retirement funds currently hold approximately $95 billion in financial assets. But with the exception of the extraordinary rescue mission recently performed by various New York State funds, retirement systems have invested in taxable securities with rates of return that are higher than tax-exempt interest rates.

The potential additional demand for tax-exempt securities is significant. For the last few years, the annual flow of funds into public retirement systems has exceeded $10 billion. Channeling even a small part of this into tax-exempt securities could have a substantial impact on borrowing costs. Moreover, there would be a net gain in the efficiency of the tax expenditure provided through tax exemption because other investors would receive lower windfall gains or would transfer their investments into the taxable market.

The pension fund subsidy is an ingenious way of getting around the problem of preserving the tax-exempt security, but it has certain drawbacks. By singling out a certain group of investors, it gives the appearance of favoritism—a problem that is admittedly more political than economic. Although the objection could be removed if private pensions were included, the administrative detail could then become burdensome. Another, more fundamental problem in this proposal is the very real possibility of self-dealing between parent governmental units and their pension funds. Such purchases would have to be monitored carefully or prohibited entirely.[15]

BOND INSURANCE OR GUARANTEES

Another family of assistance programs is designed to address the more narrow problems faced by some borrowers who have serious credit problems and urgently need capital in order to prevent further erosion and decay. These programs are based on a guaranty plan that assures investors of the timely repayment of their loans.

To be successful, these plans have to provide for the interposition of a strong credit between the borrower and lender. If such programs are successful, interest costs will be lowered as investors reduce their required risk premiums. But the risk does not disappear; it is merely shifted from one source (investors) to another (guarantor).

Programs to boost credit are usually aimed at problem

borrowers—small unknown units, highly innovative projects with no history for evaluation, or, most recently, large urban centers with depleted debt capacity and shaky cash flows. To enable such units to compete, a number of insurance or guaranty-type plans have been established.

STATE PROGRAMS OF CREDIT ASSISTANCE

State-sponsored bond "insurance" ranges from "weak" forms, based on expressions of intent to support the debt-service payments if future legislatures so elect, to "strong" forms that place the full faith and credit of the state behind the issue. Moral obligation bonds—a weak form of insurance—have been discussed earlier. Strong forms apply some insurance principles by limiting the exposure of risk to the state and charge premiums for the insurance. Two examples of this type are the Minnesota Bond Guaranty Fund and the California Health Facility Construction Loan Insurance program (see Table 15).

The Minnesota plan charges eligible borrowers a premium of 2.5 percent of principal. Eligible credits include all bond issues payable from unlimited ad valorem taxes, that is, all general-obligation bonds. Combined debt service on outstanding guaranteed bonds is limited to 20 times the amount in the guaranty fund and in authorized state municipal aid bonds.

The California plan restricts loan insurance to projects approved for construction of health facilities. Insured projects must pay an annual insurance fee that is no greater than one-half of 1 percent of outstanding principal. In the event of default, the state of California will protect investors by paying required debt service or by substituting an equivalent amount of state general-obligation bonds.

Similar strong forms of credit assistance are used to finance school construction. Approaches vary from full state assumption of the debt burden, as in Maryland, to the pledge of state aid for debt-service expenses incurred by local school districts, as in New York (see Table 16).

Table 15 Examples of Strong State Insurance Programs for Municipal Bonds

	MINNESOTA BOND GUARANTY FUND	*CALIFORNIA HEALTH FACILITY CONSTRUC-TION LOAN-INSURANCE*
Security	State has contractual obligation to guarantee repayment of principal and interest by depositing necessary funds to make up any deficiencies to payment agent prior to due date.	After default occurs, state has contractual obligation to cure default by payment of required funds or by substituting securities of equivalent amount. Such securities will be backed by full faith and credit of state.
Eligibility	All issuers of general-obligation bonds in Minnesota.	All issuers of bonds for approved health facilities in California.
Fee	2.5 percent of principal or $1,000, whichever is higher, payable at issue.	No more than 0.5 or 1.0 percent of principal outstanding in any one year, payable annually.
Other Features	Security rests upon proceeds of guaranty fees. State is also authorized to sell up to $20 million in general-obligation state municipal aid bonds to cover demands placed on fund. Principal and interest of insured bonds cannot exceed 20 times balance available to guaranty fund. Fund is not general obligation of state.	Ultimate security rests upon full faith and credit of state.

Source: Municipal Finance Officers Association, *Planning for Research on Improving Municipal Credit Quality*, Appendix, November 1974.

Private Bond Insurance   Two guaranty, or insurance, programs have originated in the private sector.[16] To qualify for private insurance coverage, municipal issues must generally be able to win an investment grade rating on their own merits. Premiums range between 0.5 and 1.5 percent of principal and interest and are based on an assessment of the default risk. Issuers or underwriters of eligible bonds may then elect to purchase an "insurance policy" that gurantees timely payment of principal and interest. Premiums are paid at the time of sale, and bonds are issued with an irrevocable insurance policy attached.

Besides the resources of the insured communities, the insurance companies place their own capital and premiums behind their pledge of payment. The insured issues of the Municipal Bond Insurance Association (MBIA) have attracted an Aaa rating from Standard & Poor. This high rating and the underlying strength of the consortium members have combined to make the program successful. From its inception in May 1974 through December 1975, MBIA has issued insurance policies for 133 issues with a par value exceeding $570 million.[17]

Table 16 Credit Assistance Programs for Financing School Construction

---

MICHIGAN SCHOOL BOND LOAN FUND

Under the state constitution, "if for any reason any school district will be or is unable to pay the principal and interest on its qualified bonds when due, then the school district shall borrow and the state shall lend to it an amount sufficient to enable the school district to make the payment." The loans are financed from the proceeds of general-obligation bonds issued by the state.

MARYLAND

Under a statute passed in 1971, the state will issue its own general-obligation bonds to finance virtually all costs of school construction.

MAINE SCHOOL BUILDING AUTHORITY

In 1969, the state constitution was amended to allow the authority to issue lease-rental bonds and to pledge the full faith and credit of the state. In addition, if a school district becomes delinquent in its lease-rental payments, the state department of education shall make state aid payments directly to the authority.

FLORIDA STATE BOARD OF EDUCATION

Under a 1972 constitutional amendment, the state board of education will issue school bonds bearing the full faith and credit of the state. Repayments are derived from an irrevocable pledge of the first proceeds of the state motor vehicle license tax.

VIRGINIA PUBLIC SCHOOL AUTHORITY

The purpose of the authority is to use the proceeds of bond sales to lend funds to localities for school construction. The bonds are initially payable from loan repayments, which are scheduled to exceed debt service. However, the Literary Fund of the Commonwealth, which also makes loans to localities, has transferred its loan notes to the reserve fund of the authority. The sum of repayment from authority loans and Literary Fund loans is estimated to cover by 1.67 times the authority's debt service.

NEW JERSEY ADDITIONAL STATE AID BONDS

Under Chap. 177 of the Laws of 1968, school districts may be entitled to additional state school building aid up to $25 per pupil. This building aid can be used only for debt service. Bonds issued under this program are payable from annual state appropriations for debt service which are paid directly to the paying agent.

NEW YORK, INDIANA, AND PENNSYLVANIA SCHOOL AUTHORITIES

Each of these states has a withholding provision. These provisions require an appropriate state official to redirect state aid payments from localities to the paying agent or the building corporation in the event that localities default on their debt-service or rental obligations.

Sources: *S&P Fixed Income Investor*, August 25, 1973, p. 608 (Maryland); *Moody's Municipal Manual*, 1974, p. 1500 (Maine); p. 1121 (Florida); p. 1120 (Virginia).

Federal Guarantees   Direct interest subsidies and bond insurance offer investors de facto protection against default. Other proposals introduced in Congress would give explicit federal guarantees to securities issued by state and local governments. In March 1968, for example, Congressman Wright Patman and Senator William Proxmire introduced identical bills to establish a government corporation, patterned on the Federal Deposit Insurance Corporation, that would guarantee payment of interest and principal on the bonds of state and local units.[18] More recently, a number of insurance or emergency loan guarantees were proposed as solutions to financial crises such as the one in New York and the credit erosion that demoralized the tax-exempt marketplace as a result.[19]

While no across-the-board guarantee programs for state and local securities have come close to enactment, a number of special-purpose measures have. The oldest and best known is the federal guarantee of housing and urban renewal bonds and notes. The Department of Housing and Urban Development has long been charged with administering federal assistance to local housing authorities and urban renewal agencies. As part of that assistance, the local agencies issue short-term project notes or long-term bonds to provide funds for low-rent housing and urban redevelopment. These tax-exempt securities are secured by the full faith and credit of the federal government and are implemented by a pledge of annual contributions sufficient to meet all debt-service obligations of the local agencies.[20]

These housing programs have been important demanders of funds in the tax-exempt market. Between 1970 and 1975, for example, more than $3.6 billion in bonds and $25 billion in urban renewal notes were issued. By June 30, 1975, more than $13 billion in guaranteed loans were outstanding.[21]

Congress has recently enacted a plethora of loan guarantee programs aimed at special purposes and involving both taxable and tax-exempt securities. In June 1976, President Ford signed into law a measure permitting the federal guarantee of leases that underlie tax-exempt pollution control bonds sold on behalf of small businesses. Soon thereafter, Congress passed bills to provide loan guarantees for constructing plants that convert solid waste to energy, for financing public facilities relating to the development of energy in coastal areas and synthetic fuel plants, and for raising the local share of payments for sewage treatment facilities.[22] And as noted in Chapter 4, HUD has developed a new coinsurance plan to assist the various state housing agencies in their marketing problems. A major attraction of the guarantee, of course, is that it requires no immediate outlay of federal money. But the federal agencies pick up large contingent liabilities that may have to be paid off if the projects fail or that may be heavily subsidized in order to prevent their failure.[23]

The Treasury has generally opposed extensions of federal backing to tax-exempt securities on the basis that the federal government would be encouraging the growth of securities that not only are a prime tax shelter but compete with, and are superior to, the Treasury's own taxable securities. In other words, the reduced costs to state and local governments are "purchased" at the price of higher costs on federal taxable securities and foregone tax revenues.[24]

SUPPORTING THE MUNICIPAL SECONDARY MARKET

Previous chapters have enumerated the factors that adversely affect the liquidity and marketability of municipal bonds. Small issues, for example, generally trade at lower prices in the secondary market, as do those of certain large, frequent borrowers with large volumes of floating debt. And the tax treatment of municipals combined with sudden shifts in bank demand add to the price uncertainty of outstanding bonds.

One solution that has been advanced would amend Section 14B of the Federal Reserve Act in order to permit the Federal Reserve System to hold state and local debt as well as obligations of the United States government.[25] The Federal Reserve has a history of opposition to most efforts to have it purchase securities other than general obligations of the federal government. Nevertheless, there is precedent for liberalizing this policy in the Board's 1966 action permitting limited repurchase agreements for federal agency securities, a more indirect means of monetizing some forms of private debt held by the agencies. Such preferential practices are sometimes used by central banks in other countries to encourage socially desirable investment and to keep private money markets from having too much influence.[26]

Amending Section 14B would have the advantage of immediately increasing the marketability of municipal bonds without congressional appropriations or additions to the federal budget. A disadvantage is inherent in the structure of the present tax-exempt market: the large number of small issues would make it difficult for the Federal Reserve trading desk to carry out open market operations in municipals without unduly influencing market conditions for particular issues or issuers. Furthermore, political pressures in favor of certain markets could develop that would further divert the attention of the Federal Reserve from its primary task of carrying out national monetary policy.

Another approach to secondary market assistance would be to develop a support device analogous to the secondary mortgage market conducted by the Federal Home Loan Mortgage Corporation, the Federal National Mortgage Association, and the Government National Mortgage Association.[27] In periods of tight credit, the assisting agency could offer to purchase a specified amount of outstanding bonds held by institutions by awarding commitments to bidders willing to accept the lowest price for their securities. To finance these purchases, the agency would market its own taxable securities.

In practice, this concept differs little from Urbank, but there is one notable exception: the secondary market agency would deal with tax-exempt issuers on an impersonal and indirect basis, especially if such purchases were conducted with recourse to the selling institution in the event of default. Theoretically, such an agency could provide a much needed escape valve against the cyclical ups and downs of the tax-exempt market. And, if successful, the attendant stabilization of prices should redound to the benefit of all issuers and investors.

CHANGING TAX LAWS TO STIMULATE DEMAND

Most proposals to improve the tax-exempt market involve government purchase of municipal securities or some form of direct subsidy to issuers or low-tax-bracket purchasers. An alternative approach calls for the federal government to eliminate impediments in the tax laws that inhibit many individuals and corporations from investing in tax-exempt municipal bonds.

Eliminating such obstacles would help make tax-exempt bonds a more efficient subsidy to state and local governments and would lessen the inequities between persons and institutions in the same tax brackets. Lowering interest rates on new and outstanding tax-exempt bonds could also lead the federal government to offer a more generous subsidy to state and local governments when proposing other arrangements to improve the market for municipal securities.

Changes in the tax laws to permit the development of unit mutual funds for municipal bonds into regular mutual funds have already been discussed. Another change might be to permit deductions for borrowing and investing in mutual bonds. This practice is disallowed under the Internal Revenue Code of 1954.[28]

Nonbank underwriters and dealers are most affected by this because their inventories of tax-exempt bonds return less income than the cost of the debt to finance these inventories. As a result, nonbank intermediaries must price new issues at anticipatory levels when future increases in interest rates are expected; this practice makes rates rise even faster. In recent testimony before the House Ways and Means Committee, the Securities Industry Association stated the case for equal tax treatment on the deduction of interest:

> We ask the Committee to permit nonbank municipal securities dealers to deduct interest expense for the purpose of carrying inventory. This tax treatment would not be different than that currently accorded commercial banks which are permitted to deduct all interest expenses even though a portion of that expense may be attributable to carrying inventories of municipal securities. Applying the same tax treatment to municipal securities dealers would increase competition between dealer and bank underwriters and lower interest costs to state and local government borrowers.[29]

REMOVAL OF RESTRICTIONS ON COMPETITION

A large proportion of bonds on the municipal bond market are sold on a competitive basis.[30] This means that unless there are poor market conditions or difficult financings, most bond issues are awarded to those underwriters that submit the highest bid (therefore, the lowest interest cost) for the bonds. Moreover, studies of the municipal bond marketing process have demonstrated that the larger the number of bids received, the better will be the price for the bonds.[31]

However, an important restriction prohibits full competition in the bidding for state and local government revenue bonds. Under the Glass-Steagall Act of 1933, commercial banks are effectively barred from underwriting and dealing in revenue bonds, though they may underwrite and deal in general-obligation securities.[32] Although some isolated exceptions have been allowed, attempts to lift this restriction have failed, primarily because of the steadfast opposition of the securities dealers.[33]

The major arguments in favor of permitting bank entry into the underwriting of revenue bonds are economic. Proponents of the change believe that the added competition would result in an increased number of bids and lower borrowing costs. Various studies of the subject indicate that, on the average, bank underwriting might lead to a savings of 5 to 10 basis points because of the added number of bidders.[34] Other factors might also lead to savings. At present, banks enjoy certain advantages with respect to the financing of municipal bond inventories. Furthermore, such an expansion of underwriting services might complement other bank services to investors and issuers, lowering per-unit distribution costs and increasing convenience.[35]

Those who oppose removal of the prohibition have their own array of arguments. They feel that such an action would heighten possible conflicts of interest in bank activities as underwriters and as investment advisors and fiduciaries. They also contend that revenue bonds are inherently more risky and thus less suitable for bank underwriting. But the most fervent objection is based on the belief that bank entry into revenue bond underwriting would destroy smaller dealers and lead to an eventual reduction in competition in the markets and, correspondingly, to a harmful agglomeration of economic power to the banks.[36]

The estimated savings resulting from the entry of banks into revenue bond underwriting would not be large on individual issues: the savings in interest for a $10 million issue enjoying a reduction of 10 basis points in interest cost would be $10,000 annually. However, with $10 billion in revenue bonds enjoying such a savings, the total reduction in annual interest costs would run $10 million, which would be multiplied by the number of years the bonds were outstanding.

INDUCED OR MANDATED INVESTMENTS

One means of raising demand for tax-exempt securities would be to allow commercial banks to count part of their municipal holdings as legal reserves.[37] A selective reserve asset policy of this type has several advantages. Because municipal securities would be more useful to bank portfolios, commercial banks would be induced to stabilize their purchases of them and to credit a proportion of these issues to meet reserve requirements during periods of tight money. This would help offset the disruptive effects of tight credit and would enhance the value of municipals above the residual status they now enjoy.

A limited move in this direction has been advocated by past members of the board of governors of the Federal Reserve System as a means of mitigating the undesirable side effects of restrictive credit conditions. The specific recommendation would permit commercial banks to use "any sound asset"— including municipal bonds—as collateral for borrowing from the discount window.[38]

The use of municipals as legal reserves would be particularly beneficial in improving the lending capacity of smaller banks. A recent Federal Reserve System committee advanced changes in the administration of the discount window to encourage borrowing by small banks, and its proposals were moved by this observation:

> Some of the smaller, more isolated banks do not, and in considerable measure cannot, effectively tap [sources of short-term liabilities]. Such banks therefore tend to hold a sizable proportion of their assets in liquid form and as a

result may be providing less credit to their communities than would be desirable.[39]

Smaller banks do not have the capability in liability management that larger banks have. In order to reduce their exposure to risk, they therefore tend to have proportionately larger holdings of U.S. Treasury notes than the larger institutions.

Counting municipals as reserve assets would, in effect, reduce the amount of monetary reserves required of banks by the Federal Reserve. Of the 13,000 banks in the United States, some 7,000 are not members of the Federal Reserve System. They represent about 20 percent of the assets of the commercial banking system and would be heavily affected by such a decision. Many of these smaller banks are presently discouraged from becoming members of the system because of Federal Reserve requirements, which are more stringent in some cases than requirements of state banking authorities.

Using the reserve mechanism of the Federal Reserve to substitute state and local obligations for federal debt would not require a costly and bureaucratic mechanism. It would not jeopardize the historic right of state and local governments to sell tax-exempt bonds—a jealously guarded prerogative that has thwarted many efforts to broaden and improve the market for municipal securities. And it would be a voluntary system—each bank would decide whether or not to invest in municipals under such a scheme.

Mandated investment in municipal securities is also being given increasingly serious attention. The prospect of non-market allocation of credit appalls many economists and most members of the business community. Nevertheless, mandated investments are a way of life in most other countries, and they exist in the thrift industry and elsewhere in this country. An example is the widespread practice of pledging. The vast majority of states and the federal government now require that financial institutions pledge or collaterize public deposits with securities of the federal government and its agencies or with state and local government securities.[40] One effect of pledging requirements is to tie the demand for eligible collateral to the level and growth of public deposits. The evidence, although sparse, suggests that these collateral requirements have had a significant effect on the borrowing costs of all governmental units. Yields on long-term municipal bonds in states with the most stringent pledging requirements average 12 basis points lower than yields on bonds from states with no pledging requirements.[41] Thus, precedent does exist for increasing demand for state and local debt instruments through legislation that effectively mandates investment policies. And reformers continue to press for additional measures along these lines.

In April 1975, the New York State Assembly held public hearings on a proposal to establish a state bank. The bank would serve as a depository for public funds and could invest in loans to municipalities, to other community organizations and projects, and even to small businesses.[42] The impetus for the hearings was the belief that financial intermediaries had failed to provide sufficient funds to help solve the seemingly intractable problems of urban centers. The idea of a state bank thus reflects an opinion that investments in projects with high social priority could be mandated by a state legislature.

REDUCING THE SUPPLY OF TAX-EXEMPT SECURITIES

Because, in most cases, tax exemption lowers borrowing costs, it is extremely attractive to borrowers of large sums. But the supply of money seeking tax shelter at any given interest rate is limited. When the demand for such financing is heavy, competition among borrowers serves to raise interest rates and reduce the benefits of the tax exemption. Conversely, reductions in the supply of tax-exempt bonds improve the market for those that remain.

Most proposals to improve the municipal market are designed to stimulate total demand. Another approach derives from the view that the market is now overburdened by borrowings that cannot be justified in terms of their public purpose. If these could be purged, so goes this reasoning, the market for eligible borrowings would thereby be enlarged.

The use of the public's credit to finance ventures and facilities for profit-making enterprises has been attacked throughout our history. But it is not easy to draw the line between proper and improper uses of tax exemption. Many of the businesses that benefit from such financing are engaged in activities—such as pollution control or the construction of housing or hospitals—that are generally considered as meeting important social needs. Still, the easy use of public credit to finance private projects is increasingly coming under fire. A forceful illustration of this was the recent testimony by the Securities Industry Association before the House Ways and Means Committee:

The easy use of public credit to finance private projects is increasingly coming under fire. A forceful illustration of this was the recent testimony by the Securities Industry Association before the House Ways and Means Committee:

> This committee can act to reduce municipal borrowing costs and increase the efficiency of the tax-exempt market by returning the market to the exclusive use of public state and local government issues. We ask this committee to eliminate private pollution control and industrial development financing from the tax-exempt market.[43]

As discussed in Chapter 3, several other applications of tax-exempt financing have been criticized. Especially questionable is the use of advanced refunding bonds, which can lead to a multiplication of outstanding tax-exempt debt for a particular project.[44] Refunding—that is, selling new bond issues to replace outstanding ones at the time they mature or are called in—has been used traditionally to overcome restrictive conditions on the original loan, to reduce interest costs, or to stretch out debt-service payments. Advanced refunding differs from straight refunding in that such bonds are sold prior—sometimes many years prior—to the date of the issue that they are meant to replace. The proceeds of the sale are then held in escrow until the original bonds mature or are eligible to be called. Because the old issue and its replacement are outstanding at the same time, the supply of tax-exempt bonds can be inflated to a multiple of the amount actually needed to finance the original improvement.[45]

There are two major objections to the use of advanced refunding in tax-exempt securities. First, in the past, the device has been used for the sole purpose of earning the issuer a profit by investing the escrow account in taxable securities that earn a return in excess of the cost of borrowing. This objection, however, was largely removed by provisions of the 1969 Tax Reform Act. Now, by a quirk in the regulations, the profits can only be enjoyed by a third party—usually the banker or lender that provides for the escrow account. The existence of the third-party profit has, unfortunately, encouraged the promotion of advanced refundings by those who stand to profit, even when the refinancing may represent little or no gain to the issuer.[46]

A second objection to advanced refunding arises from increases in the supply of tax-exempt securities without comparable increases in the funds available for public improvements. The added supply of tax-exempt bonds keeps tax-exempt yields from being as low as they otherwise might be. Furthermore, advanced refundings become much more attractive when rates decline, and thus, the potential of the supply acts as an overhang on the market and keeps it from recovering as quickly and completely as it otherwise might.[47]

By mid-1976, it was evident that for the municipal bond market as a whole, a reduction in the supply of tax-exempt bonds was not in the offing. The total volume of bond offerings had kept pace with the record-breaking level of 1975, and the supply of hospital and pollution-control revenue bonds continued to swell. However, the short-term market for tax-exempts was operating at a much lower level, as some issuers were blocked from the market and others chose to steer clear of short-term debt and to fund debt with long-term bonds wherever possible.[48] Tax-exempt interest rates remained high by historical standards—nearly 7 percent for good-grade long-term bonds—and investors continued to be cautious and selective. The marginal credits were filtering back into the market by one means or another—usually with trimmed-down demands for funds. The lessons of the past few years had been costly, and the municipal bond market would not soon forget them.

Appendix

A Framework for Analyzing Tax-Exemption and Federal Credit Assistance Programs and Other Actions Affecting the Municipal Bond Market

TAX EXEMPTION AS A SUBSIDY

In weighing the various proposals to assist the municipal bond market, it is important to understand how tax exemption works as a market subsidy that permits state and local governments to borrow more cheaply than taxable borrowers. Analyzing the market in terms of the supply and demand analysis will help show how tax exemption does this.[1]

Chart 1 illustrates how tax exemption influences the market for state and local bonds, how its benefits are split among the borrowers and investors, and how its costs are absorbed by the federal government. Most states and some localities with an income tax also exempt the interest income on their own and their subdivisions' securities (sometimes those of others as well). Thus, they also experience costs from foregone taxes on the subsidy.

Curve S is the supply of bonds forthcoming at each level of the tax-exempt rate (r_e): the higher the interest rate, the smaller the supply of bonds. The shape and location of the S curve are determined by several factors, but essentially, they depend on demand for capital goods by state and local governments and their sensibility to changing interest cost. These, in

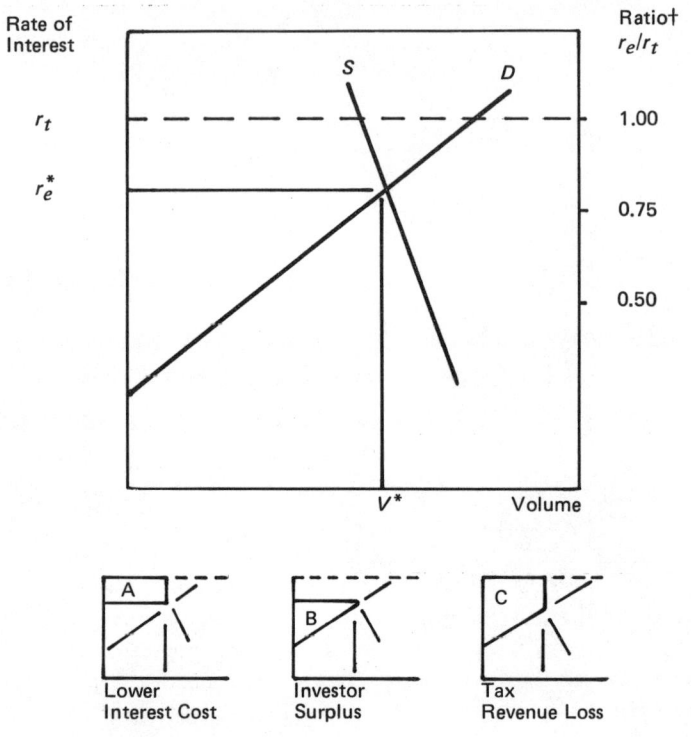

†Assume taxable interest rate is constant at r_t.

Appendix Chart 1   Tax Exemption as a Market Subsidy

turn, are highly influenced by the expectations of future price and interest levels and the availability of alternative means of financing.

Many studies have found state and local borrowing and outlays sensitive to interest rates. In the short run (one year), a 10 percent *rise* in the cost of borrowing generates a 5 to 10 percent *reduction* in borrowing, other factors varying. Capital spending seems to show a smaller impact, with an ultimate impact of a 2 percent reduction (elasticity of –0.2).

Curve D is especially important. It shows the demand for

bonds by investors at varying levels of interest. Note that if we assume the taxable bond rate (r_t) is fixed (that is, it does not change with the supply of tax-exempt bonds and is drawn as a horizontal line), then the level of r_e determines the ratio of r_e to r_t, as shown on the right-hand scale of the chart. It is also assumed that the tax-exempt and taxable bonds are alike in every respect except that the interest income on one is taxable and on the other is tax-exempt.

Investors interested in maximizing income will seek to equate *after-tax* returns on their investments so that the individual demand curve gives a tax-exempt interest rate that will lure a taxpayer into the tax-exempt market, given the taxable rate of r_t. That is, the after-tax rate of return on r_t for an investor with the marginal tax-bracket t^m equals the tax-exempt rate r_e in equilibrium:

$$r_e = (1 - t^m)r_t$$

If $r_e > (1 - t^m)r_t$, then the investor will demand more tax-exempts; if $r_e < (1 - t^m)r_t$, then he will buy more taxable bonds. Many other things will determine the individual demand curve, but here we look at the tax effects in particular. As we sum all these demand curves together for individual investors, we find the shape of the market demand curve. In reality, the aggregate demand curve D is a complex function of marginal tax brackets, income, wealth, portfolio objectives, and alternative investment possibilities. But, focusing on the tax effects, note that it follows that the vertical distance between D and r_t gives the marginal tax rate of the investor groups at each level of r_e^* that would just clear the market (expressed as $1/t^m = r_e^* = r_t$).

Examining the intersection values, we find a r_e^* will match the D and S curves at volume V^*. And assuming a fixed taxable rate of interest, this, in turn, implies a ratio of r_e^*/r_t and an equilibrating marginal tax bracket of t^{m^*} for the market. At those values, the area labeled A in the insert at the bottom of Chart 1 gives the amount of interest saved because issuers borrowed tax-exempt at r_e rather than at r_t. This savings will be enjoyed each year the bonds are outstanding, the debt bargain having been struck for the life of the bonds. Concurrently, the lost tax revenue, area C, will be equal, annually, to the taxes investors would have paid had they bought taxable bonds instead of tax-exempts in the same amount and earned the taxable rate of r_t on them. This is equal to areas A plus B. Area B is the volume of tax-sheltered income absorbed by investors that is *not* passed on to state and local borrowers.

Although there are several complications that can be introduced into the analysis, the crux is that as the supply of bonds increases (as curve *S* moves right), lower-tax-bracket investors are brought into the market and area B (investor surplus) increases in proportion to area A (interest-cost reduction). In the extreme, the tax-exempt and taxable markets merge at r_t; area A goes to zero and area B becomes equal to the area C subsidy cost—all of it flowing to investors!

Two important things should be noted. First, r_e and r_t are assumed to be the rates of return on investments that are perfect substitutes, except for the marginal tax rate of the investor. But many experts argue that tax-exempts are not equivalent to taxables (primarily because of a thin secondary market) and would need a higher rate if sold on a taxable basis. Second, investors do have alternative tax shelters that will attract investable funds instead of taxable bonds. Both these arguments mean that a higher taxable rate is required than that implied by a simple comparison between r_t and r_e.

There have been several efforts to measure the size of the taxes avoided (the Treasury cost) relative to the reduction in interest cost and the net benefit to investors. Most recent estimates put the cost of the tax-exempt subsidy on all outstanding debt at $4.8 billion, of which $3.5 billion goes to reduced interest costs and $1.3 billion is retained by investors in the higher bracket. The ratio of the reduction in state and local interest cost to Treasury tax losses is thus calculated to be 73 percent. (Other estimates place it at 70 to 75 percent.)[2] However, for new borrowings occurring in any given year, the subsidy can vary greatly, depending on market conditions. This ratio can be viewed as a measure of the efficiency of tax exemption—that is, the proportion of the subsidy that goes to the intended beneficiary, the state and local governments.

It is also clear that the efficiency is closely tied to the equity problem. Equity can be defined as having taxpayers pay tax on their economic income at the stated marginal rate *or*, in the case of tax exemption, inducing them to transfer an amount that is equivalent to their foregone taxes to governmental issuers in terms of reduced interest costs (that is, "pay the tax" by lowering the return they get on municipal bonds in the same amount as the foregone taxes). Obviously, to the extent that the market clears at interest rates that imply a lower marginal rate than the top rate, then the "equity" of the progressive tax is being eroded (that is, area B grows relative to area A).

EVALUATION OF ALTERNATIVE MARKET ASSISTANCE MECHANISMS

Analytically, all forms of assistance (or reforms) can be examined to discover how they work on either the demand or supply side of the market. However, they may vary greatly in terms of the institutional mechanisms and procedures used.

The leading alternatives for assistance have been discussed elsewhere in this study. Briefly, they are: (1) taxable bond option, allowing governments to choose voluntarily between selling a bond on a tax-exempt or taxable basis with a subsidy; (2) agency direct loans, whereby an agency of the government (Urbank) sells taxable bonds and uses the proceeds to acquire tax-exempts; (3) loan guarantee or insurance, under which the federal government or an agency puts its guarantee—with or without a fee—behind the borrower; (4) increasing the attractiveness of tax exemption, which involves a variety of tax code changes to stimulate the demand for municipal bonds by encouraging additional investors to enjoy more tax exemption; and (5) reducing the supply of tax-exempts by restraining certain uses of tax exemption by law (such as pollution control bonds).[3]

Although the taxable bond option and federal credit programs operate differently in their administration (Urbank requires a new institution, whereas taxable bonds do not require this), they are practically identical from the standpoint of demand and supply analysis.

Chart 2 is like Chart 1 except that now a new horizontal line at interest rate r_s has been added. The difference between r_t and r_s is a subsidy of the interest rate. Thus, at a 40 percent subsidy, the net cost to borrowers would be $r_s = (1 - 0.40)r_t$. Obviously, for the option to be used, r_s must be less than r_e, the initial market clearing rate. As the option is used, the market rate is driven to $r_e^* = r_s$, the new equilibrium rate. (Urbank, an alternative to a market subsidy, could achieve the same result if it were willing to lend to anyone at a posted lending rate of r_s.)

As the rate drops, the volume of municipals sold increases from V to V''. Note that at r_s, a total of V'' tax-exempt bonds would continue to be sold, while $V_s - V''$ taxable bonds would be sold.

Appendix Chart 2   Effect of Direct Taxable Subsidy (at rate of Subsidy S, where $r = (1 - S)r_t$)

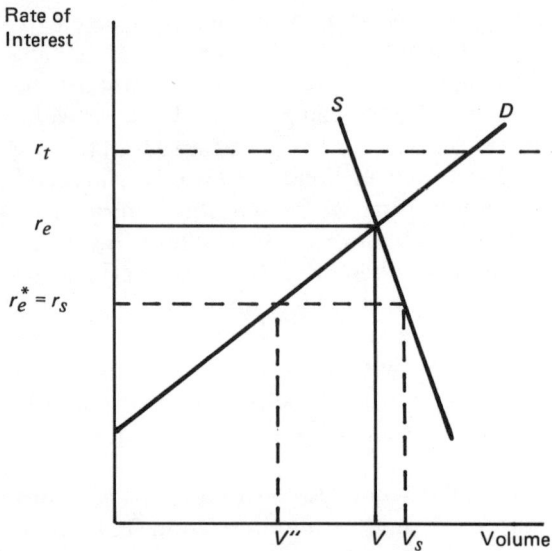

Chart 3 gives a graphic depiction of the costs and benefits of the subsidy (outside of administrative costs). The most salient point is that the net cost of the subsidy to the Treasury would be small compared with the reduction in interest cost for state and local governments. By reducing the supply of tax-exempts, the subsidy also lowers the rate on them (to r_s), thus improving the efficiency of tax exemption and reducing the tax shelter provided. This is a side benefit from the subsidy.

Appendix Chart 3 Itemized Effects of Subsidy (as depicted in Appendix Chart 2)

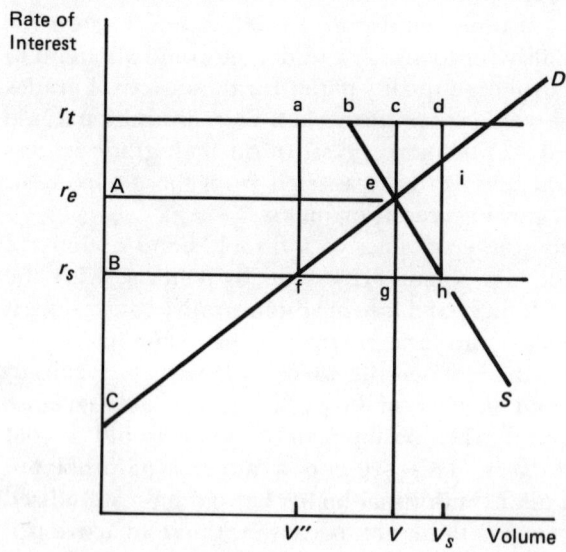

ITEM	AREA
Benefits: lower interest costs	ABge + iegh
increased borrowing	$V_s - V$
Costs to Treasury: subsidy outlay	adhf
Minus increased tax revenues	adif
Equal net outlay	fih
Reduction in investor surplus	ABfe
Remaining investor surplus	CBf

In itself, the subsidy is efficient in lowering the cost to governments that elected to sell taxable securities. Beyond that, since it lowers the supply of tax-exempts, the subsidy also improves that efficiency of the remaining bonds sold without the subsidy and as tax-exempts.

The all-important factors in the taxable bond option (or an Urbank) are the voluntary nature and the level of the subsidy. If governments are indeed free to sell bonds at r_s (which is r_t minus the subsidy), they will sell taxables when the tax-exempt rate exceeds r_s and tax-exempts when the tax-exempt rate is below r_s. The big drawback of the Urbank is its institutional nature; it abandons a market bidding situation and by administrative action would post a rate (or set of rates) for those who qualify for loans. In addition, it would also tend to substitute its own high-quality paper for the variety of grades that otherwise would enter the market. This substitution would probably tend to put more pressure on high-grade issuers and in general remove those assisted from the discipline of distinctions regarding creditworthiness.

Obviously, the economics of a taxable bond option are attractive, and its problems are essentially political. Were the option truly voluntary and free of administrative constraints, it would lower state and local borrowing costs. The higher the subsidy ratio, the greater the savings. However, a subsidy beyond the mid-40 percent range would probably collapse the tax-exempt market inasmuch as all bonds would be sold on a taxable basis. This presents a number of problems. Should the bulk of municipal bonds be sold on a subsidized basis? Most analysts think not, because without an active primary municipal bond market, the state and local governments would be captives of a direct federal subsidy. Another problem is the degree to which society wants to subsidize the government's use of capital, thus diverting it from private uses. Also, a radical change in capital market values for outstanding bonds means large capital gains for the present holders of tax-exempt bonds. In summary, sharp changes can so distort existing relationships that predictions of results are hazardous.

SOME COMPARATIVE ANALYSES

There is a broad range of actions open to the federal government that will have various effects—or none at all—on municipal borrowing arrangements. Ultimately, the desirability of assistance programs or of other actions such as changes in the tax code depends on establishing a set of criteria (or policy targets) and seeing how each proposal stacks up against the requirements.

Table 1 offers a nonrigorous but helpful comparison of advantages and disadvantages of actions regarding the municipal bond market viewed from two different perspectives. One set of criteria focuses on lowering the cost of borrowing and on preserving independence of decision making at the state and local governmental levels. The second set concerns the efficiency and equity of a subsidy program, matters of particular interest to the federal government.

Factors of importance to state and local governments are:

Lower borrowing costs: the ability of proposals to reduce cost and stabilize interest rates, generally, to municipal borrowers (+) or, conversely, to raise them (−).

Federal involvement: the degree of need for federal approval or appraisal of a borrower's plans and creditworthiness; (+) shows little or no involvement, (−) relatively more involvement.

Fiscal and market discipline: whether or not assistance preserves (+) or erases (−) basic credit distinctions and keeps the assisted borrower in a competitive primary market for his debt.

Impact on Nonassisted: the degree to which those not directly assisted are either helped (+) by a reduction in supply or are relatively penalized (−) if not eligible for assistance (leapfrogging weaker ahead of stronger credits).

Appendix Table 1 Pluses and Minuses of Various Federal Credit Assistance Techniques and Changes in Tax Treatment of Municipal Bonds

	TAXABLE BOND OPTION	URBANK (AGENCY) LOAN	GUARANTEED TAXABLE BOND	PENSION FUND SUBSIDY	INSURANCE OR GUARANTEE OF TAX-EXEMPTS	MUTUAL FUND PASS-THROUGH	REDUCING SUPPLY OF TAX-EXEMPTS
Impact on state and local governments							
Lower borrowing costs	++	++	++	+	+	+	+
Federal involvement	0	–	–	0	–	0	–
Fiscal and market discipline	0	–	–	0	–	0	0
Impact on non-assisted	+	+	+	+	–	0	+
Total	3	1	1	2	–2	1	1
Impact on federal government							
Administrative cost and complexity	0	–	–	–	–	0	0
Efficiency of subsidy	+	+	+	+	–	0	+
Tax equity	+	+	+	+	–	0	+
Helps needy more	0	+	+	0	+	0	0
Total	2	2	2	1	–2	0	2
Combined totals	5	3	3	3	–4	1	3

Factors of importance to the federal government are:

Administrative cost and complexity: the degree to which the assistance requires institutions and procedures for administration and the cost thereof; (−) denotes more and (+) denotes less complexity and cost.

Efficiency of subsidy: how much of the gross subsidy outlay is passed on to the intended beneficiary (i.e., borrowers), as opposed to being leaked to others. A more efficient subsidy gets (+), a less efficient gets (−).

Tax equity: how much the assistance increases (−) or reduces (+) the available shelter from federal income taxes.

Help to needy borrowers: the degree to which the mechanism favors (+) those governments most in need from an "ability to pay" perspective or handicaps (−) them.

Any such list is highly subjective. Some would add entries of their own, such as whether or not the plan involves anything except a direct tax-exempt issuance. Others would focus on the federal budgetary impact: Does the assistance appear as an outlay, or can it be hidden somewhere off the balance sheet or as a foregone tax receipt? More controversial than the particular components on the list is how to weight the factors in scoring an assistance plan.

Various assumptions have been made in the development of this illustrative set of pluses and minuses, the basic assumption being that the assistance plan is designed to work in good faith. For example, it is assumed that a taxable bond or an Urbank provides a 30 to 40 percent subsidy on taxable borrowings (direct or via an agency), that a guarantee is a federal guarantee, and that insurance premiums are designed to cover administrative cost but not individual economic risks (a flat rate). Also, it is assumed that the proposals are constitutionally sound and efficiently administered.

Double symbols have been used to represent roughly the anticipated magnitude of the impact of the changes. Where there seems no appreciable difference from the situation with the conventional tax-exempt market, there is a zero (0). In all cases, the *comparison is with the situation as it now exists* through exclusive reliance on tax-exempt securities and the subsidy these entail.

The exercise illustrated in the appendix table makes explicit the major trade-offs in the design of assistance programs and other actions affecting the municipal bond market. Direct market subsidies and loans at preferential notes and terms have the biggest impact on borrowing costs. But any action that generally reduces the supply of tax-exempt bonds, upgrades their credit quality, or enhances the demand for them will tend to do the same. Conversely, those programs that increase the supply of such bonds or give preferential treatment to selected classes of tax-exempt borrowers, given the demand for bonds, tend to raise the costs for others. Moreover, selective assistance programs call for federal involvement, add to the program's administrative cost and complexity, and can erode fiscal discipline. Similarly, more restrictions on the supply of bonds mean a curtailment of privileges by federal action.

From the federal perspective, programs that reduce the supply of tax-exempts have favorable effects on the efficiency and equity of tax exemption, although they may or may not be aimed at those groups considered most in need. Perhaps the most remarkable conclusion is that most assistance programs and many other actions can result in an overall improvement from both the state and local government and the federal government standpoints.

Notes

Chapter 3

[1]State and local governments had total receipts from all sources of approximately $209 billion in 1974, of which $44 billion represented federal grants in aid. Little, if any, of the federal money is available for debt service. Furthermore, of the $165 billion raised by states and localities, much is earmarked for certain purposes. For example, nearly $14 billion of the receipts from all sources was specifically assigned to social insurance programs, mainly employee retirement plans and unemployment insurance. Therefore, any comparisons of the sector's total burden of debt with total receipts must be tempered by the facts that only a portion of the revenues is available for such purposes and that relationships can vary greatly among the individual 78,000 state and local units now in existence.

[2]Figures from various issues of the Investment Bankers Association's *Statistical Bulletin* and the Securities Industry Association's *Municipal Market Development*.

[3]For a discussion of such devices, see John E. Petersen, *Changing Conditions in the Market for State and Local Government Debt,* a study for the Joint Economic Committee, U.S. Congress (April 16, 1976), chapter 2.

[4]See Lennox Moak, *Administration of Local Government Debt* (Chicago: Municipal Finance Officers Association, 1970), pp. 17–18.

[5]For most varieties of revenue bonds, the reoffering yields have been 15 to 20 basis points (1/100 of a percentage point) higher than general-obligation bonds of similar credit rating. See George Hempel, *The Postwar Quality of State and Local Debt* (New York: National Bureau of Economic Research, 1970), pp. 142–144.

[6]For a study of the origins of the lease-rental bond and its relationship to the growth of statutory authorities, see William E. Mitchell, *The Effectiveness of Debt Limits on State and Local Borrowing* (New York: New York University Institute of Finance, 1967).

[7]Public Law 90-364, sec. 107, 90th Cong., June 28, 1968, as amended October 24, 1968.

[8]There is widespread underreporting of pollution control bonds and other industrial development bonds. A recent survey by the Governments Division, U.S. Bureau of the Census, placed underreporting of pollution control

bonds at approximately $300 million in 1974. See Maurice Criz and David Kellerman, "Unlisted Pollution Control Debt via IDB's Held Exaggerated," *Daily Bond Buyer,* June 22, 1976, pp. 18–19.

[9]George Peterson and Harvey Galper, "Tax-Exempt Financing of Private Industry's Pollution Control Investment," *Public Policy,* spring 1975. See also Peter Fortune, "The Financial Impact of the Federal Water Pollution Control Act: The Case for Municipal Bond Reform," Harvard Institute for Economic Research, 1975.

[10]John E. Petersen, "The Tax Exempt Pollution Control Bond," Municipal Finance Officers Association, *Analysis,* March 1975, pp. 4–5. See also Peterson and Galper, op. cit., p. 33.

[11]In June 1976, President Ford signed legislation authorizing the Small Business Administration to provide federal guarantees of tax-exempt bonds issued for pollution control purposes by small businesses.

[12]Petersen, "The Tax Exempt Pollution Control Bond," pp. 6–7.

[13]Of 71 financings rated by Moody's in 1975, 52 hospitals had insufficient net current revenues to meet peak expected debt service. See *Moody's Bond Survey,* January 5, 1976, p. 1795.

[14]Michael Geczi, "Hospital Borrowing via Tax-Exempts Soared to High in '75," *Wall Street Journal,* January 19, 1976, p. 21.

[15]The Senate Finance Committee introduced legislation in June 1976 that would extend the ceiling on tax-exempt industrial revenue bonds from $5 million to $20 million for private hospitals. See *Daily Bond Buyer,* June 16, 1976, p. 19.

[16]Alan Bautzer, "Stadium, Civic Center Projects Flourish Despite Fact Most Are Losing Propositions," *Daily Bond Buyer,* May 24, 1976, p. 759.

[17]Ibid.

[18]"State Housing Agencies: Roles and Accomplishments" (Council of State Housing Agencies, April 1975), p. 2.

[19]"State Housing Agencies," *Housing and Development Reporter* Supplement, November 10, 1975, p. 50.

[20]For an account of the creation of the moral obligation, see *Restoring Credit and Confidence,* a report by the New York State Moreland Commission, March 31, 1976, pp. 108–115.

[21]For a discussion of the mechanics of the moral obligation, see *Moody's Bond Survey,* September 17, 1973, pp. 568–569.

Chapter 4

[1]Alan Bautzer, "New York Agency's Insolvency Shakes Markets," *Money Manager,* March 3, 1975, p. 1.

[2]*Moody's Bond Survey,* January 12, 1976, p. 1765.

[3]See statement of William J. White in *Debt Financing Problems of State and Local Governments: The New York City Case, Hearings before the House Committee on Banking, Currency and Housing,* October 22, 1975, pp. 1361–1368.

[4]Remarks by Ronald Forbes, "State Aid to Local Government," Panel 3, National Governors Conference, Washington, D.C., February 24, 1976.

[5]"HUD Unveils Program to Coinsure State HFA Mortgages," *Daily Bond Buyer,* June 11, 1976, p. 1.

[6]*Federal Register,* June 17, 1976, pp. 24678–24680.

[7]*Restoring Credit and Confidence* (see note 20, Chapter 3), p. 20.

[8]See Ronald Forbes and John E. Petersen, "Costs of Credit Erosion in the Municipal Bond Market," Municipal Finance Officers Association (revised, December 1975), p. 17. See also Stephen Chilton et al., "Trends in Short Term Borrowing Costs for New York State Localities" (Albany: State University of New York, December 1975).

[9]John E. Petersen, *The Rating Game: Report of the Twentieth Century Fund Task Force on Municipal Bond Credit Ratings* (New York: Twentieth Century Fund, 1974), pp. 125–126.

[10]U.S. Congress, Joint Economic Committee, *New York Financial Crisis,* November 1975, pp. 11–15.

[11]Roy Bahl et al., "The Impact of Economic Base Erosion, Inflation, and Employee Compensation Costs on Local Governments," Paper 23, Maxwell School, Syracuse University, Syracuse, New York, September 1975, p. 2.

[12]*New York Financial Crisis,* pp. 19–21.

[13]*Boston Globe,* December 22, 1975, p. 1.

[14]Bahl et al., op. cit., pp. 23–24.

[15]Thomas Muller, *Growing and Declining Urban Areas: A Fiscal Comparison* (Washington, D.C.: Urban Institute, 1975).

[16]Between 1965 and 1972, states increased their relative share of combined state and local revenues by only 2.2 percent and of expenditures by only 1.3 percent. See Bahl et al., op. cit., p. 28.

[17]Federal Reserve Board, *Flow of Funds* (various issues).

[18]U.S. Congress, Joint Economic Committee, *The Current Fiscal Positions of State and Local Governments,* 1975, pp. 28–29.

[19]Muller, op. cit., pp. 56–59.

[20]James Howell, "Economic Maturity: Choices and Costs," *Balanced Growth for the Northwest* (New York State Senate, 1975), pp. 50–55.

[21]"Where the Funds Flow," *National Journal,* June 26, 1976, p. 889.

[22]George Peterson, "Finance," in William Gorham and Nathan Glazer (eds.), *The Urban Predicament* (Washington, D.C.: Urban Institute, 1976), pp. 43–49.

[23]Ibid., pp. 72–79.

[24]"The Second War Between the States," *Business Week,* May 17, 1976, p. 92.

[25]"Where the Funds Flow," pp. 881–885.

[26]For example, see the industrial development recommendations of the New York State Moreland Commission, *Restoring Credit and Confidence* (see note 20, Chapter 3), pp. 50–55.

Chapter 5

[1]Paul Schneiderman, "State and Local Government Gross Fixed Capital Formation: 1958–73," *Survey of Current Business,* October 1975, p. 18.

[2]Surveys by the Federal Reserve Board have plotted the reaction of the state and local sectors to tight money in 1966, 1969, and 1970, as well as behavior in periods of relative ease. See Paul F. McGouldrick and John E. Petersen, "Monetary Restraint and Borrowing and Capital Spending by Large State and Local Governments in 1966" and "Monetary Restraint and Borrowing and Capital Spending by Small Local Governments and State Colleges in 1966," *Federal Reserve Bulletin,* July and December 1968, respectively. See also John E. Petersen, "Response of State and Local Governments to Varying

Credit Conditions," *Federal Reserve Bulletin,* March 1971; and Harvey Galper and John E. Petersen, "Strengthening the Municipal Bond Market," *Investment Dealers Digest,* October 20, 1970, pp. 7–8.

[3]Harvey Galper and George Peterson, "The Equity Effects of a Taxable Municipal Bond Subsidy," *National Tax Journal,* December 1973, pp. 611–624.

[4]Schneiderman, op. cit., p. 19.

[5]Ibid., p. 26. As of the first quarter of 1976, state and local construction expenditures were running about $2 billion below those of the same period in 1975.

[6]Barry Bosworth, James S. Duesenberry, and Andrew S. Carron, *Capital Needs in the Seventies* (Washington, D.C.: Brookings Institution, 1975), p. 36.

[7]Ibid., pp. 56–57.

[8]*The Financial Outlook for State and Local Governments to 1980* (New York: Tax Foundation, 1972).

[9]*Special Analysis,* The Budget of the U.S. Government for Fiscal Year 1976, 1975, p. 69.

[10]David Ott and Attiat Ott, *State-Local Finances in the Last Half of the 1970s* (Washington, D.C.: American Enterprise Institute, 1975), pp. 95–98.

[11]Fortune, op. cit. (see note 9, Chapter 3), Table 7.

[12]Steven Taylor, "A Financial Background for Project Independence," Board of Governors of the Federal Reserve System, mimeographed, 1974, pp. 15–16.

[13]Bosworth et al., op. cit., p. 69.

[14]Taylor, op. cit., Table 15.

Chapter 6

[1]Robert Heufner, *Taxable Alternatives to Municipal Bonds,* Research Report No. 53 (Federal Reserve Bank of Boston, 1972), p. 125.

[2]While maximization of returns to shareholders is a generally accepted goal for most private enterprise, the need to maximize after-tax income is especially critical for banks. Bank lending capacity is tied to capital in several ways. National banks, for example, are limited in the amount of unsecured credit that can be extended to any one borrower to 10 percent of capital and "free" surplus. A popular ratio for analyzing bank conditions at present is the ratio of "scheduled" or problem loans to bank capital. While this measure can be misleading, it does illustrate the highly levered nature of commercial banking and the impetus to improve capital position.

[3]Prior to the Tax Reform Act of 1969, banks were allowed to net capital gains and losses from securities transactions, to deduct net losses from ordinary income, and to apply lower capital gains tax rates on net gains. This led to "tax swapping" as banks attempted to establish net losses or gains in particular years. Portfolio switches were profitable in two ways. First, banks received a larger stream of tax-exempt income from the higher coupons. In addition, the sale of more seasoned issues at a discount gave rise to capital losses that were fully deductible from before-tax income. Any capital gains realized as interest rates subsequently declined were taxed at the (lower) capital gains rate. The Tax Reform Act reduced incentives to banks to engage in tax swapping by declaring that capital gains would henceforth be taxed at ordinary rates.

[4]See Frank Morris, statement before the House Committee on Ways and Means, Panel No. 8, *An Alternative to Tax-Exempt State and Local Bonds,* February 23, 1973, p. 29.

[5]The growth of time deposits in general and of certificates of deposit (CDs) in particular is the result of two complementary forces. On the one hand, rising rates of inflation and higher interest rates have induced individuals and corporations to reduce their holdings of nonearning assets. Commercial banks have been able and willing to accommodate these portfolio adjustments, and Federal Reserve policy generally has encouraged accommodation. Reserve requirements, for example, are much lower on time than on demand deposits. The growth of CDs was also enhanced early on by the increase in the maximum rate payable under Regulation Q of the Federal Reserve to 5.5 percent in 1965. Temporarily unconstrained by the fetters of Regulation Q, banks actively bought funds by paying the going price in the money market. Regulation Q was subsequently applied as an effective tool for monetary control in 1966 and 1969, but in 1970, ceilings on the short-term (less than 80 days) certificates were suspended, and ceilings on all other large CDs were suspended in 1973.

[6]In the spring of 1970, the Internal Revenue Service tried to challenge banks on the deductibility of interest on time deposits. However, the dramatic impact of this challenge on the municipal market, as well as its potential effect on bank earnings, led the IRS to back off. It declared in July 1970 that such interest expenses shall remain tax deductible for indebtedness they incur in the ordinary course of their day-to-day business, unless there are circumstances demonstrating a direct connection between the borrowing and the tax-exempt investment. A direct connection will be deemed to exist in certain circumstances—for example, if certificates of deposit were issued to a state in exchange for tax-exempt obligations having maturity dates approximately the same as the certificates of deposit. (IRS, Technical Information Release No. 1039, July 21, 1970.)

[7]The Bond Buyer, *1975 Municipal Finance Statistics,* June 1976, p. 22.

[8]From the standpoint of tax accounting, the use of accelerated depreciation in leveraged leasing leads to higher recorded depreciation expenses and "book losses" from specific project financings that can be used to offset taxable income flows from other bank assets. However, the after-tax cash flow available for reinvestment is increased as a result, because recorded depreciation on accounting statements is a noncash expense. The investment tax credit also increases after-tax cash flows because it provides for an outright reduction in tax liabilities.

[9]Donald J. Mullineaux, "The Taxman Rebuffed: Income Taxes at Commercial Banks," Federal Reserve Bank of Philadelphia, *Monthly Review,* May 1974, pp. 19–20.

[10]"Problem Loans Haunt the Banks," *Business Week,* January 26, 1976, p. 23.

[11]As noted by Mullineaux, more than 87 percent of investment tax credits, 70 percent of depreciation deductions, and 98 percent of foreign tax credits claimed by all commercial banks were claimed by banks with assets of more than $100 million in 1970.

[12]*1975 Municipal Finance Statistics.* Bank holdings declined by another $800 million between December and June 1975 and then rebounded by $1.8 billion at the end of 1975. However, some of this increase was involuntary— the result of the New York note moratorium—and even then, holdings remained below 1972 levels.

[13]Elizabeth Hobby, *Maturity Distribution of Obligations of States and Political Subdivisions Held by Insured Commercial Banks, June 30, 1972,* Federal Deposit Insurance Corporation, p. 8.

[14]One effect of the most recent portfolio shifts carried out by money-center banks has been to highlight the emerging role of smaller banks as mainstays in the municipal market. Over the period 1972 to 1974, for example, banks with less than $100 million in deposits increased net purchases of municipals by $7.2 billion, or 75 percent of the total increase in bank holdings during the period.

[15]Brian Fabbri made some comments on the first half of 1975: "The bank takedown of the massive recession-inspired Treasury financing reached 54.3%, and it is expected that banks will continue to take down a similarly large portion of the anticipated future Treasury debt. As this materializes, bank holdings of Treasury securities are expected to reach $80 to $90 billion, or perhaps, very close to their World War II peak of $90.2 billion. Another interesting consequence of the present exceptionally large bank takedown of Treasuries is the break from the postwar cyclical pattern of bank acquisitions and liquidations of Treasury securities. As previously mentioned, the peaks and troughs in bank holdings of Treasuries had been lower in each successive cycle over the period. However, the current peak in Government holdings far exceeds all six peaks in bank ownership of Governments over the postwar period." *Commercial Bank Investments in the Postwar Period* (New York: Salomon Brothers, 1975), p. 27.

[16]Heufner, op. cit., pp. 172–174.

[17]The survey was conducted by Ronald Forbes of the Municipal Finance Study Group, State University of New York at Albany, and reported in John E. Petersen, "The Tax Exempt Pollution Control Bond."

[18]Tom Herman, "Auto Insurance Rates to Rise 13%–20% This Year, Mostly Because of Inflation," *Wall Street Journal,* January 21, 1975, p. 25.

[19]Salomon Brothers, "Fire and Casualty Industry: Earnings Review," December 5, 1975, p. 4.

[20]Galper and Peterson, op. cit. (see note 3, Chapter 5), p. 617.

[21]Data on a personal income refer to adjusted gross incomes of which at least part was taxable at the marginal rate. See U.S. Internal Revenue Service, *Statistics of Individual Income Tax Returns.*

[22]"Bond Funds Sell $2.5 Billion," *The Bond Buyer,* January 12, 1976, p. 1.

[23]Cited in E. H. Davis, "Municipal Bond Investment Funds," in U.S. Congress, Joint Economic Committee, *State and Local Public Facility Needs and Financing,* vol. 2, p. 416. (Emphasis added.)

[24]As summarized by Davis (ibid., p. 419): "A sponsor finds it necessary to accumulate and hold during a period of several months a large part of the municipal (public) bonds which will form the portfolio for the next series of a municipal investment fund. The sponsor may gain or lose on the portfolio accumulation phase of the operation because the value of the bonds on the date of deposit with the trustee may be greater or less than cost. When the series is created, the sponsor-underwriter is exposed to risk of financial loss during the period when such series is being distributed. The risk of financial loss while holding units is, to some extent, even greater than while holding the bonds by reason of the fact that the offering price is inflexible (under the terms of the trust indenture the public offering price of units is defined as a price 'equal to the offering price per unit of the bonds in the fund plus a sales

charge of 4½% of the public offering price'). Thus the sponsor-underwriter cannot terminate its exposure by distributing units at retail at a price differing from that produced by application of the formula."

[25]John Winders, "First Tax-Exempt Mutual Fund to Be a Limited Partnership," *Weekly Bond Buyer,* May 3, 1976, p. 1.

[26]Kemper Municipal Bond Fund, Ltd., Registration Form S-5, filed with the Securities and Exchange Commission, p. 6.

[27]See statement of Robert L. Augenblick on behalf of the Investment Company Institute, *Proposals Relating to Tax Exempt Bonds, Hearings before the House Committee on Ways and Means,* January 22, 1976.

Chapter 7

[1]In part, the relatively smaller dollar size of municipal issues reflects the almost exclusive reliance of state and local governments on public offerings for capital, even when they need small amounts of money. Business firms, on the other hand, carry out private placements through negotiations with commercial banks, life insurance companies, and other institutional investors.

[2]In the week of November 10, 1975, for example, an analysis of some 27 competitive issues showed that 14 different maturity structures were utilized in these issues, with final maturities ranging from 6 to 40 years. The number of coupon rates per issue ranged from a single coupon (on an issue with 29 maturities) to 14 different coupon rates.

[3]In an analysis of 35 bond issues offered during the summer of 1973, offering statements were compared for completeness on 24 specific categories of credit information. This study showed that several types of important credit data were reported in only 10 percent of the cases. See Ronald Forbes, Arthur Hierl, and John E. Petersen, "Assessing the Value of Credit Information in the Municipal Bond Market," paper presented at the annual meeting of the Financial Management Association, October 1974.

[4]As James Duesenberry has expressed it, "We may say that the operating efficiency of capital market institutions is satisfactory if they perform their functions at minimum cost. That requires that (1) their expenditures should be as low as possible given the results that they achieve and that (2) profits should be high enough to attract capital in sufficient volume to permit them as a group to expand with the economy but no higher. The capital markets may be said to operate in a satisfactory way when borrowers are not rationed except by price and when there are no interest rate differentials except those due to risk differentials and differentials in placement and servicing cost by size and type of loan or borrower and those due to geographical differences." "Criteria for Judging the Performance of Capital Markets" in H. Wu and A. Zakon (eds.), *Elements of Investments* (New York: Holt, 1972).

[5]A thorough exposition of criteria that enter into the determination of appropriate debt structures is offered in Moak, op. cit. (see note 4, Chapter 3).

[6]Yields on bonds of different maturities are generally higher the longer the period to the final payment date. This yield-to-maturity relationship reflects the fact that investors are exposed to more difficulties or adverse movements in interest rates the longer the maturity of their investment. However, the slope of the yield-maturity curve fluctuates, and there are occasions when short rates are higher than long rates. This represents another determinant

of the yield-to-maturity schedule—investors' expectations of future interest rates. For a thorough discussion, see Burton Malkiel, *The Term Structure of Interest Rates* (Princeton, N.J.: Princeton University Press, 1966).

[7]Portfolio managers are also vitally concerned with maintaining adequate diversification so as to reduce risks of losses from unexpected default or difficulties with any specific credit. Thus, the variety of bonds in the market is not without its benefits if they are of economical size. However, studies suggest that relatively few different issues are required for diversification by reducing unique risks attached to specific securities. (By far the largest element of risk is systematic risk—the fact that all credits are exposed to general economic conditions—a risk that cannot be diversified in any way.) For a review of portfolio theory, see Jack Francis and Stephen Archer, *Portfolio Analysis* (Englewood Cliffs, N.J.: Prentice-Hall, 1971), pp. 154–158.

[8]Several studies have commented on the variability of municipal bond rates relative to interest rates on other fixed-income securities. Diller, for example, detected seasonal patterns, and Smith and Marcis found evidence of a pronounced seasonal movement in municipal bond rates in all maturities. See Stanley Diller, *The Seasonal Variation of Interest Rates* (New York: National Bureau of Economic Research, 1969), and V. Kerry Smith and Richard G. Marcis, "A Time Series Analysis of Post-Accord Interest Rates," *Journal of Finance,* June 1972, pp. 589–605.

[9]Roland Robinson, *Postwar Market for State and Local Government Securities* (Princeton, N.J.: Princeton University Press, 1960), p. 129.

[10]Reuben Kessel, "A Study of the Effects of Competition on the Tax-Exempt Bond Market," *Journal of Political Economy,* July-August 1971, pp. 706–738.

[11]Michael Hopewell and George Kaufman, "Commercial Bank Bidding on Municipal Revenue Bonds: New Evidence," forthcoming in the *Journal of Finance.*

[12]There are fewer bids on revenue bonds because commercial banks cannot underwrite them except in the special cases of housing, health, and university bond issues. See, for example, Hopewell and Kaufman (ibid.) and Chapter 9 of this paper.

[13]Kessel, op. cit., pp. 710–716.

[14]These and other advantages are discussed at somewhat greater length in Robert E. Toolan, "The Bond Bank—How It Works and Where It Is Going," Municipal Finance Officers Association, *Special Bulletin,* September 1972.

[15]Municipal Finance Study Group, "The Vermont Municipal Bond Bank: A Promising Innovation," *Daily Bond Buyer,* February 22, 1971, pp. 18–19.

[16]Several states have centralized borrowing for specific purposes, usually educational. Maine, Pennsylvania, Georgia, and Virginia use special borrowing authorities, and Maryland finances local school construction directly through the state. Insurance and debt-service subsidy programs are also used. See Petersen, *The Rating Game* (see note 9, Chapter 4), pp. 137–138.

[17]Municipal Finance Study Group, op. cit., p. 18.

[18]Recommendations for improved forms of assistance are found in *State Technical Assistance to Local Debt Management* (Washington, D.C.: Advisory Commission on Intergovernmental Relations, 1965).

[19]David R. Berman and Lawrence A. Williams, "Credit Problems of Small Municipalities," *State and Local Public Facility Needs and Financings,* a study for

the Joint Economic Committee, U.S. Congress, December 1966, vol. 2, pp. 249–250.

[20]John E. Petersen, "Response of State and Local Governments to Varying Credit Conditions," *Federal Reserve Bulletin,* March 1971, pp. 219, 224.

[21]An efficient secondary market can be described as one with depth, breadth, and resiliency. A market has depth when there are bid and offer prices above and below the existing price. It has breadth when there are a large number of buy and sell orders, and it has resiliency when these orders come into the market with small fluctuations in price. In the analytical jargon of economists, a secondary market with breadth, depth, and resiliency is characterized by elastic demand and supply schedules. For a thorough discussion of the implications of depth, breadth, and resiliency, see David Fand and Ira Scott, Jr., "The Federal Reserve System's 'Bills Only' Policy: A Suggested Interpretation," *Journal of Business,* January 1958, pp. 12–18.

[22]A thorough description of the roles performed by dealers and brokers is provided by John J. Kenny, "The Secondary Market in Municipal Bonds," in *State and Local Public Facility Needs and Financing,* vol. 2 (Washington, D.C.: U.S. Government Printing Office, 1966), pp. 227–230. See also William Staats, "The Secondary Market for State and Local Government Bonds," in *Reappraisal of the Federal Reserve Discount Mechanism,* vol. 3 (Washington, D.C.: Federal Reserve Board of Governors, 1972), pp. 1–24.

[23]*Securities Acts Amendments of 1975,* Report of the Committee on Banking, Housing and Urban Affairs, U.S. Senate, April 14, 1975, p. 43.

[24]As noted by SEC Commissioner John R. Evans in recent congressional testimony, these estimates overstate the number of dealers who actively participate in transactions of volume, because listed dealers include small banks whose dealer operation exists "only for the purpose of buying for their respective bank portfolios at dealer prices." See *Trading in Municipal Securities, Hearings before the Subcommittee on Securities of the Senate Committee on Banking, Housing and Urban Affairs,* May 1974, p. 62. As another indicator of the number of active dealer participants, information on trading income from secondary-market transactions in municipal bonds is available for registered securities firms earning more than $20,000 a year in gross revenues. These data do not include commercial bank dealers. Of the $217 million total income reported by the approximately 625 firms with municipal bond trading revenues in 1971, 25 percent was earned by the 5 largest nonbank dealers and approximately 84 percent was earned by the 100 largest firms.

[25]Robinson, op. cit., p. 123; and Securities Acts Amendments of 1975, op. cit., p. 40.

[26]The *Blue List* has a number of shortcomings as an indicator of trading volume. Advertised dealer inventories, for example, are generally acknowledged to represent only a fraction of actual inventories. Moreover, new issues are often listed on a when-issued basis—that is, before the securities have been issued and delivered—as a tactical move by dealers to "plumb" the depth of the market. Finally, the listed "ask" prices or yields may bear little resemblance to the market clearing price that would cause a transaction to take place. See Kenny, op. cit., and Robinson, op. cit., pp. 122–126, for a full discussion of these points.

[27]Robinson, op. cit., p. 125.

28K. Larry Hastie, "Determinants of Municipal Bond Yields," *Journal of Financial and Quantitative Analysis,* June 1972, pp. 1729–1748.

29There are good reasons to expect that the dealer segment of the secondary market is fairly efficient: "First, it is a professional market, national in scope. From the information that is generally available, it seems clear that significant changes have been taking place in this market over the last decade. Brenton Harries has noted that the number of subscriptions to the *Blue List,* the most complete published record of offerings, has increased from 2,975 in 1960 to 5,404 in 1972; the number of firms advertising bonds out for bids has increased from 617 to 745 over the same period. Concomitantly, technological improvements in communications (e.g., WATS lines, private teletype systems, and remote computer terminals) have accelerated the dissemination of information and have permitted dealers to 'screen' much larger quantities of information in a much shorter period of time. These trends—the growing number of dealers and the use of improved information systems—imply gains in operating and allocative efficiency for the municipal secondary market." Ronald Forbes, "Some Observations on Yield Differentials in the Municipal Secondary Market," in *Proceedings,* Eastern Finance Association, 1973 Annual Meeting, pp. 57–63.

30See John McCallum, "The Impact of the Capital Gains Tax on Bond Yield," *National Tax Journal,* December 1973.

31The exposition of these practices and their effects is contained in Michael Hopewell and George Kaufman, "Costs to Issuers of Using NIC in Competitive Bond Sales," *Daily Bond Buyer, MFOA Supplement,* June 24, 1974. As Hopewell and Kaufman point out, the current method for awarding bids assumes that borrowers do not have any preferences for the timing of their total interest payments but are concerned only with the total amount to be paid. This can lead to the acceptance of economically "wrong" bids as well as higher interest rates due to inefficiently designed coupon structures.

32Barbara A. Brinkley, "Computing Municipal Bond Interest the Canadian Way," *Commercial and Financial Chronicle,* January 6, 1975, p. 1.

33Two exceptions are the 1975 issues sold by the Federal Home Loan Mortgage Corp. and the Pacific Power and Light Co.

34Moak, op. cit. (see note 4, Chapter 3), p. 286.

Chapter 8

1Theoretically, a widespread divulging of all the material information will provide the market with a basis for more rational decision making and reduce the inequities and inefficiencies that grow out of uncertainty and manipulation: "With full disclosure, we would expect less drastic shifts in estimates of expected profitability of a given issue as a result of the greater initial level of economic information (and presumably the reduction in the possibility of surprises from this source), a greater scope for scientific investment analysis, a diminished reliance on and use of rumors, and a reduction in the scale of manipulative practices." Irwin Friend and Edward Herman, "The SEC through a Glass Darkly," *Journal of Business,* October 1964.

2Ratings are designed for investors but are purchased by issuers. For an extensive discussion of the rating agencies and their impact on the market, see Petersen, *The Rating Game* (see note 9, Chapter 4).

[3]"An important use of ratings by underwriters is to outguess the agencies. This translates roughly into acquiring bonds that may be upgraded and avoiding bonds that may be downgraded." Peterson, *The Rating Game* (see note 9, Chapter 4), p. 15.

[4]Richard West, "Bond Ratings, Bond Yields, and Financial Regulations: Some Findings," *Journal of Law and Economics,* May 1973, pp. 159–168.

[5]Daniel Rubinfeld, "Credit Ratings and the Market for General Obligation Municipal Bonds," *National Tax Journal,* March 1973, p. 25.

[6]Because of their opinions' influence on the market, rating agencies have been the object of recurring attempts to bring their practices under some form of federal regulation. For the latest round of discussions, see *To Amend the Investment Advisor Act of 1940 to Provide for the Regulation of Persons Rating Municipal Bonds, Hearings before the House Subcommittee on Consumer Protection and Finance on H.R. 675,* June 23 and 24, 1976.

[7]Petersen, *The Rating Game* (see note 9, Chapter 4), p. 99.

[8]Ibid., pp. 1–22.

[9]Ibid., pp. 14–18.

[10]Advisory Commission on Intergovernmental Relations (ACIR), *City Financial Emergencies* (Washington, D.C.: U.S. Government Printing Office, 1973), p. 5.

[11]See the statement of the Municipal Finance Study Group, *Municipal Securities Full Disclosure Act, Hearings before the Senate Committee on Banking, Housing and Urban Affairs,* February 24–26, 1976, pp. 255–288.

[12]Ibid., p. 260. The criteria for evaluating tnese official statements were based on items included in the November 10, 1975, draft of the "Disclosure Guidelines for Offerings of State and Local Securities," published by the Municipal Finance Officers Association. The guidelines covered three broad classes of credit information, including (1) a timely and comprehensive statement of outstanding indebtedness, (2) a detailed financial report, including the revenues and expenditures and the balance sheet of the borrower, and (3) a thorough report of the economic and demographic characteristics of the population served by the governmental unit.

[13]Ibid., pp. 264–266.

[14]ACIR, *City Financial Emergencies,* pp. 67–68.

[15]Gordon Calvert (ed.), *Fundamentals of Municipal Bonds,* Securities Industry Association, 1972, p. 2.

[16]George Hempel, *Postwar Quality of State and Local Debt* (New York: National Bureau of Economic Research, 1971), p. 21.

[17]W. Braddock Hickman, *Corporate Bond Quality and Postwar Experience* (New York: National Bureau of Economic Research, 1958), pp. 122, 126.

[18]ACIR, op. cit., p. 22.

[19]Hempel, op. cit., p. 28.

[20]Robert Doty and John Petersen, "The Federal Securities Laws and Transactions in Municipal Securities," pp. 77–82 (forthcoming in *Northwestern University Law Review*).

[21]Statement of Thomas Masterson, "Trading in Municipal Securities," pp. 154–218.

[22]John Petersen and Robert Doty, "Regulation of the Municipal Securities Market and Its Relationship to the Governmental Issuer," Municipal Finance Officers Association, *Analysis,* December 1975.

[23]The board can require dealers to supply only such information about issuers that is generally available from a source other than the issuer. See Section 15B(d) (1) and (2) of the 1934 Securities and Exchange Act.

[24]Although the amendments forbid the direct or indirect requirements for review of issuer documents prior to sale, they remain subject to antifraud provisions. As the Senate report on the legislation noted, "The bill assures that access of state and local governments to the capital markets will not be regulated in ways not now permitted under the fraud provisions of the Federal securities laws." Senate Report No. 94–75; *Securities Act Amendments of 1975*, p. 47.

[25]The antifraud provisions include Section 17 of the Securities Act of 1933 and Section 10(b) of the Securities and Exchange Act of 1934.

[26]The exemptive language had been of lesser concern during the formulation of regulation. What objections there were came late, and the subject of controls over issuer information was never broached in the hearings on municipal bond market regulation. Thus, at the time of passage, Congress went on record as saying that the power for such controls was not to be possessed by the Rulemaking Board and was circumscribed in the case of the SEC. *Hearings before the House Committee on Interstate and Foreign Commerce on H.R. 4570*, March 1975.

[27]Robert J. Cole, "Holding Municipal Bonds up to the Light," *New York Times*, October 26, 1975, section 3, p. 1. Charles N. Stabler, "Creditable Cities?" *Wall Street Journal*, January 6, 1976, p. 1.

[28]Late in 1974, bills to this effect were introduced by Senator Thomas Eagleton (S. 2574) and Congressman Lionel Van Deerlin (H.R. 10522 and 10523).

[29]See *Municipal Securities Full Disclosure Act*. The hearings focused on the bill introduced by Senators William and Tower, S. 2969, which was supported by the SEC and, with reservations, by the Treasury. (See pp. 18–42.)

[30]See Lennox Moak, statement before the Committee on Banking, Housing and Urban Affairs, U.S. Senate, October 9, 1975.

[31]ACIR, *City Financial Emergencies*, p. 15.

[32]Robert Doty, "The Case for Municipal Self-Regulation," *Daily Bond Buyer*, January 29, 1976, p. 2.

[33]See Petersen and Doty, op. cit., and "Suggested Guidelines for Disclosure and Municipal Bond Offerings," Municipal Finance Officers Association, November 10, 1975, draft.

[34]Linda Greenhouse, "Carey Is Urging a Disclosure Law," *New York Times*, June 6, 1976, p. B4.

[35]ACIR, *State Technical Assistance to Local Debt Management* (see note 18, Chapter 7), pp. 23–45.

[36]Petersen, *The Rating Game* (see note 9, Chapter 4), p. 13.

[37]Petersen, *The Rating Game* (see note 9, Chapter 4), p. 13.

[38]For a summary of state data collection and advisor services, see John Petersen, "State Assistance in Local Government Credit Information and Disclosure Activities," in *Municipal Securities Disclosure Requirements for Insurers and Underwriters* (Philadelphia: American Law Institute–American Bar Association, 1976), pp. 155–168.

[39]For a discussion of the distinctions between governmental and business accounting principles, see Edward Lynn and Robert Freeman, *Fund Accounting Theory and Practice* (Englewood Cliffs, N.J.: Prentice-Hall, 1974), pp. 1–12.

[40]The generally accepted governmental accounting principles are authoritatively set forth in *Governmental Accounting, Auditing and Financial Reporting*, National Council on Governmental Accounting, 1968, and *Audits of State and Local Governmental Units*, American Institute of Certified Public Accountants, 1974. These principles are modified from time to time by pronouncements of the publishing organizations and by pronouncements of the Financial Accounting Standards Board.

[41]Petersen, "State Assistance in Local Government Credit Information and Disclosure Activities," pp. 163–166.

[42]Ibid., pp. 158–161.

[43]Ibid., pp. 155–158, 163–167. See also ACIR, *City Financial Emergencies*, Appendix E.

[44]Securities Industry Association, "Municipal Market Developments," February 1976, pp. 1–3. In 1975, evidence indicated that North Carolina bonds sold on an average of about 40 basis points lower interest cost than the national average and about 30 basis points better than those of the surrounding states in the Southeast.

Chapter 9

[1]See Harvey Galper and John E. Petersen, "An Analysis of Subsidy Plans to Support State and Local Borrowing," *National Tax Journal,* June 1971. For a more general analytical treatment of interest subsidy plans, see also Rudolph Penner and William Silber, "The Interaction between Federal Credit Programs and the Impact on the Allocation of Credit," *American Economic Review,* December 1973, pp. 838–852.

[2]The history of the TBO is detailed in Heufner, op. cit. (see note 1, Chapter 6). An extensive discussion of its operation is found in Committee on Ways and Means, U.S. House of Representatives, Panel No. 8, *An Alternative to State and Local Tax-Exempt Bonds,* February 23, 1973.

[3]U.S. House of Representatives, Committee on Ways and Means, *Taxable Bond Alternatives for State and Local Governments,* March 29, 1976. Current legislative proposals range from a 30 percent subsidy to one of 40 percent. Higher subsidy levels have been discarded because of their possible perverse effects on the bond markets and tax equity. (See note 5 below.)

[4]Statement of Peter Fortune, *Federal Financing Authority, Hearings before the Senate Committee on Banking, Housing and Urban Affairs,* May 17, 1972, p. 230.

[5]Galper and Peterson, op. cit. (see note 20, Chapter 6), pp. 621–623. Galper and Peterson calculate that 48 percent is the logical upper limit on the subsidy ratio for a variety of reasons and that prudence would argue for stopping short of that level.

[6]Statement of Peter Fortune, op. cit., p. 231.

[7]See Committee on Ways and Means, *Taxable Bond Alternatives,* pp. 12–13. The net cost to the Treasury (excess of subsidy cost over increased tax receipts) rises from $6 million with a 30 percent subsidy, to $45 million with a 40 percent subsidy, to $150 million with a 50 percent subsidy, for the first year the plan is in operation. At the end of 10 years, the annual costs would be roughly 12 times the first year's cost.

[8]Ibid., pp. 13–14. The Ways and Means Committee staff estimated that a 35 percent subsidy would reduce interest costs of state and local governments in the first year of its operation by $157 million, of which $99 million is a direct

subsidy and $58 million is a general reduction in tax-exempt interest rates. This is about 7.4 times the Treasury's estimated net cost of $21 million in the excess of subsidy payments over increased tax receipts.

[9]U.S. House of Representatives, Municipal Taxable Bond Alternative Act of 1976, House Report No. 94-1016, April 7, 1976, pp. 18–23. The Ways and Means version had the blessings of Treasury, but because of a lack of broad support, the bill was never brought to the floor of the House for a vote.

[10]Statement of Wallace O. Sellers, *Alternatives to Tax-Exempt State and Local Bonds, Hearings before the House Committee on Ways and Means,* January 21–23, 1976, p. 51.

[11]Statement of William J. Reynolds, ibid., p. 158.

[12]See Galper and Petersen, "An Analysis of Subsidy Plans," p. 23.

[13]Advisory Commission on Intergovernmental Relations, *Federal Approaches to Aid State and Local Capital Financing,* September 1970, p. 32.

[14]Harvey Galper and John E. Petersen, "Strengthening the Municipal Bond Market," *Investment Dealers Digest,* October 20, October 27, and November 3, 1970.

[15]The investment policies and other aspects of public employee pension funds have been coming in for criticism recently. See U.S. House of Representatives, Committee on Education and Labor, *Interim Report on Activities of the Pension Task Force,* March 31, 1976, pp. *v–vii;* and Louis M. Kohlmeier, *Conflicts of Interest: State and Local Pension Fund Asset Management* (New York: Twentieth Century Fund, 1976).

[16]Municipal Bond Insurance Association (MBIA) and American Municipal Bond Assurance Corporation (AMBAC).

[17]*Daily Bond Buyer,* January 6, 1976, p. 15.

[18]See *Financing Municipal Facilities, vol. 2, Hearings before the Joint Economic Committee,* July 9, 10, and 11, 1968, pp. 169–188.

[19]See *New York City Financial Crisis, Hearings before the Senate Committee on Banking, Housing and Urban Affairs,* October 9, 10, 18, and 23, 1975.

[20]A concise description of these programs is provided in First Boston Corp., *Handbook of Securities of the United States Government and Federal Agencies,* 25th ed., 1972.

[21]See *Special Analyses, Budget of the United States Government, Fiscal Year 1977,* chapter E, "Federal Credit Agencies."

[22]See John Connor, "Senate Votes Guarantees for Energy Bonds," *Daily Bond Buyer,* June 30, 1976, p. 1. See also *Money Manager,* July 6, 1976, p. 2.

[23]See U.S. Congress, Joint Economic Committee, *The Economics of Federal Subsidy Programs,* January 11, 1972, pp. 31–35, 73–74.

[24]See U.S. House of Representatives, Committee on Banking and Currency, *A Study of Federal Credit Programs,* vol. I, February 28, 1964, pp. 146–147.

[25]"Central Bank Seen as Owner of Local Government's Issues," *Daily Bond Buyer,* February 6, 1969, pp. 1, 15; and Edward Renshaw and Donald Reeb, "A Costless Public Policy: Shared Revenues from State-Local Bonds," *Congressional Record,* February 17, 1969, pp. E1025–1032.

[26]See Lester Thurow et al., *Activities by Various Central Banks to Promote Economic and Social Welfare Programs,* a study prepared for the Committee on Banking and Currency, U.S. House of Representatives, January 11, 1971.

[27]See, for example, the Federal Municipal Credit Corporation, H.R. 7747, introduced by Congressman Mario Biaggi, June 10, 1975.

[28]Section 265(2), 1954 Code.

[29]Statement of Wallace O. Sellers, op. cit.

[30]Traditionally, approximately 95 percent of general-obligation bonds (both in number and amount) and over 50 percent of revenue bonds are sold on a competitive basis. Recently, market disruptions and more complex transactions have lowered these proportions. See Securities Industry Association, *Municipal Market Developments* (various issues), Table 4, "Type of Offering."

[31]See Chapter 7 of this paper.

[32]12 U.S. Congress. See 378(a). Commercial banks are permitted to purchase revenue bonds for their investment accounts and may participate in syndicates in which other members underwrite the bonds, but they cannot themselves reoffer or make a market in revenue securities.

[33]For a recent discussion of the controversy and its history, see Roger Mehle, "Bank Underwriting of Municipal Revenue Bonds: Preserving Free and Fair Competition," *Syracuse Law Review,* fall 1975. The latest round of debates is contained in U.S. Senate, Committee on Banking and Currency, *Trading in Municipal Securities, Hearings on S. 1933 and S. 2474,* October 16, 1973.

[34]See ibid., pp. 261–262, statement of Leland Prussia.

[35]See ibid., pp. 303–307, statement of Reuben A. Kessel.

[36]See ibid., pp. 342–348, statement of Alvin Shoemaker.

[37]Ronald Forbes, Donald Reeb, and Edward Renshaw, "How the Federal Reserve Could Help to Stabilize and Improve the Market for Municipal Bonds," *Bankers Magazine,* summer 1971.

[38]Former Federal Reserve Board governor Andrew Brimmer advocated a policy of selective reserve requirements on assets designed to raise marginal costs and reduce commercial lending by banks. This proposal can be viewed as a limited version of the Brimmer proposal in the sense that counting municipals as legal reserves has the effect of lowering conventional reserve requirements.

[39]Board of Governors of the Federal Reserve System, Report of a System Committee, *Reappraisal of the Federal Reserve Discount Mechanism,* 1968, p. 6.

[40]Although the Treasury permits a wide degree of latitude in the types of securities that can be pledged, it distinguishes between the relative value of securities by varying the percentage of face value that will be allowed. At the state and local levels, requirements vary greatly from state to state. For recent discussions of the practice, see John E. Petersen, "Full Insurance of Public Deposits and Pledging Requirements," *Analysis,* Municipal Finance Officers Association, February 1974; and Ronald Forbes, "The Effects of Pledging Requirements on the Municipal Bond Market," in *Governmental Deposit Insurance, Hearings before the Subcommittee on Financial Institutions of the Senate Committee on Banking, Housing and Urban Affairs,* March 19–21, 1974.

[41]Forbes, ibid., pp. 319–337.

[42]Alan Bautzer, "Nader, Janeway, Steingut Urge Passage of Bill to Create a New York State Bank," *Daily Bond Buyer,* April 25, 1975, p. 1.

[43]Securities Industry Association, statement before the House Committee on Ways and Means, January 21, 1975, p. 5.

[44]Lennox Moak, Outline of Statement, Testimony before the Joint Economic Committee, *Hearings on the Financial Condition of Cities,* June 20, 1975. See also Petersen, *Changing Conditions in the Market* (see note 3, Chapter 3), chapter 2.

[45]See Thomas F. Mitchell, "Municipal Bonds: Advanced Refunding," *Governmental Finance,* May 1976, pp. 45–50.

[46] Ibid., p. 49. Although the Treasury has made proposals to curb the possibility of the windfall profit, no results are yet available. See U.S. Treasury, "Proposals for Tax Change," April 30, 1973, p. 148.

[47] Between 1970 and 1974, reportedly $2.7 billion in advanced refunding bonds were sold, the week of sales occurring during the recovery period of 1971–72. See Salomon Brothers, *Supply and Demand for Credit in 1975* (New York, 1975), p. 16.

[48] "Note Financings for May Slip to $2.3 Billion," *Money Manager,* July 6, 1976, p. 41.

Appendix

[1] More extensive algebraic and diagrammatic expositions of tax exemption and various alternative borrowing subsidies are found in Harvey Galper and John Petersen, "An Analysis of Subsidy Plans to Support State and Local Borrowing," *National Tax Journal,* June 1971; David and Attiat Ott, "The Tax Subsidy through Exemption of State and Local Bond Interest," in U.S. Congress, Joint Economic Committee, *The Economics of Federal Subsidy Programs, Part 3: Tax Subsidies,* July 1972; and Robert Huefner, *Taxable Alternatives to Municipal Bonds,* Research Report No. 53, Federal Reserve Bank of Boston, 1972.

[2] "The Municipal Bond Market: Why It Needs Help," *Congressional Record,* December 17, 1975, S. 22558. See also Peter Fortune, "The Municipal Bond Market: The Need for Reform," *Tax Notes,* March 29, 1976, pp. 3–8. Fortune argues that the tax-exempt market is more efficient than commonly is inferred from comparisons of long-term tax-exempt and taxable rates, because the ratio of tax-exempt to taxable rates is typically higher in the shorter-maturity obligations.

[3] For another useful summary, see American Enterprise Institute, *Proposed Alternatives to Tax-Exempt State and Local Bonds,* February 14, 1973.